ONE

ON

O②NE

A Minute With Ben

We've got it in our heads in this country
that forgiveness is weakness. It's strength.
The hardest thing you're ever called
upon to do is to forgive --
particularly when the fault is all
on the part of the other man or woman.

What's it like to live like there's no tomorrow?
I know because I lived that way for many years. But then
one day I discovered there is a tomorrow -- and it was
really quite frightening.

I was in a restaurant. Two guys were talking in the next
booth. One asked, "Charlie, how long have you got to
live?" And Charlie replied, "Here or hereafter?"

Well, it sounded crazy at first. But then I discovered in
the Bible, if it's to be believed, that everyone lives two
lives.

The first is on earth. It's very short ... one to 100. The
second begins at the physical death on earth, and
it's forever. And that's an awfully long time.

Everyone I know is concentrating primarily on time,
but God makes time. Imagine.

Forgiven for eternity. Unforgiven for eternity. It makes
sense because God says that he's planted eternity in
every heart.

BEN HADEN
January 2013

②ONE on ONE

is visually laid out to reflect
Ben Haden's unique speaking style.
All Scripture Verses
are featured in bold print.

COPYRIGHT 2015

BEN HADEN

Scripture quotations taken from The Holy Bible, King James Version.
Scripture quotations from the New American Standard Bible®, ©The
Lockman Foundation 1960, 1962, 1963, 1968, 1971, 1972, 1973, 1975,
1977, 1995. Used by permission.

CONTENTS

Grace

Grace is not much use if you don't share it,
is it?

It's easy to read about the prodigal son
but never to dwell on
your own prodigal life.

But the same grace available
to the prodigal son
is available to us --

and to this nation
for its misdeeds, its sins,
its distance from
the only one and
true and living God.

The Cross is what
draws us.

At the Cross ...
it's all grace.

The compass

I heard of a young man who went out in weather about 10° above zero. He had on a light jacket, and he knew the area. He went out hunting ... and instead got lost. For four hours he tried to find his way.

He was afraid he would freeze to death. He had nothing to eat. Somehow he sensed he was going in circles. "God help me find my home," he cried out.

God did -- without his freezing ... without starving ... without tragedy. But you know something? Unless that young man is unlike the rest of us, you forget the incident very quickly. Even if he's lost again, he'll be terribly worried. He'll feel alone, out of touch. He'll think it's terrible ... and he can't possibly make it.

You forget that Jesus Christ is the *compass* of every life that receives Him. Is it a wondrous thing, with all our weaknesses that the Lord has given us this promise:

In no year, under any circumstance, anywhere on the face of the earth, will we be confronted with any temptation that is beyond our strength ... unless He provides an escape for us.

That's how gracious He is. That's why you can trust Him. He's built for the crisis. He is the Lord!

I will not leave you comfortless: I will come to you.

John 14:18

Have to do both ...

"I've tried to live.
I don't know how to live.
I don't know how to die --
and I have to do both."

That's right. You do.
Like it or not, you've got to do both.
Then -- how to do it? Yeah, how to do it?

My friend, you need Christ.
I don't know how much more He could love you
than to keep God's promise.

God the Son ...
coming from Heaven to earth --
to become a man,
to become my sin,
to become your sin,

to go to the Cross,
shed His blood for the forgiveness of my sin ...
and the forgiveness of your sin.
And He endured my hell for my sin ...
and your hell for your sin.

I think, my friend,
this is a Christ you'll want to trust.

If you had never been born ...

Christ wants us to be His arms, His legs, His body ... to take his physical place until He returns.

Now think, if you had never been born ... is there someone who would have remained unloved by anyone?

If you had never been born, is there someone to whom you extended forgiveness and to whom no one else has ever extended forgiveness?

Has someone been in desperate need ... a need you have uniquely met or a need that would not have been met, if you had not been born?

Christ understands all our ways intimately. He values us beyond any part of His creation. When we do His work, it is invaluable and it is costly.

In First John, the Apostle John makes this statement: **This love assures us of confidence in the Day of Judgment; the love of Christ. Because as Christ is, so are we,** (the believers) **in this world.**

I John 4:17

Question ...

What
do
guilty
people do?

       They condemn.

What
do
forgiven
people do?

       They forgive.

What is the source of the poor man's joy?

The poor, unrecognized Christian ... is recognized as a rich man because God has singled him out and died for him. That's a source of joy to the poor man.

What about the rich man? The rich man is asked to be joyful for finding something he can't buy ... he can't bargain for. He can't earn it. He can't deserve it. Suddenly he feels in low estate, rather than in the highest estate.
    "Is that healthy?" you ask.

Oh yes. The humblest of Christians I've ever known have been wealthy men ... because they knew the temptations of wealth ... how diversionary it is ... how much it leads you into thinking, "This is it!" ... rather than the Kingdom of God -- being it.

Is your disappointment in the *world*? Or is it in Christ? Have you ever gone to the Heavenly Father ... single-mindedly ... to ask Him for wisdom, a different kind of wisdom than the wisdom of this world, and been turned away? Have you found that He lied? Have you ever found that He doesn't love you?

Where are the wise? Where is the teacher of the law? Where is the philosopher of this age? Has not God made foolish the wisdom of the world?

I Corinthians 1:20

Inquiring ...

You're an inquirer today ...
you're just filled up to here
with doubt and with questions.

There's so many dilemmas
about the Christian faith
and about the person Jesus in your mind.

You wonder -- how would the Lord deal with me?

Graciously.
He will always honor honest doubt,
honest questions, honest inquiring,
honest probing.

It's the dishonest
that He will not honor.

You know the person who says:
        "I have only one question ..."
then if you answer that satisfactorily,
he's got a hundred more in the bag.

So the question they have is not honest ...
it's not the guts he's probing for.

Making more time ...

"Ben," you say, "on what would you reflect?"

I'll tell you exactly on what I would reflect.
I would make more time for my wife.
I would make more time for our only child.
I would make time for Jesus Christ.

I always found time to work ... I always found time for golf ... I always found time for poker ... I always found time for partying ... I always found time for the important conventions ... I always found time for friends. So it wasn't a question of not having time. It was -- not making time.

Have you ever noticed that we all want to be a concert pianist but without practicing -- or football stars without training?

We all want to have a good family -- but without necessarily being good to our families.
We all desire to have a close family -- but without necessarily being close to our families.

Regrets! Regrets!

To every thing there is a season, and a time to every purpose under the heaven.

Ecclesiastes 3:1

Collision course ...

If you had to be perfectly frank, would you say that as a nation and as individuals -- we're on a collision course?

You must have heard it because it's been quoted for decades. It's a lesson from history!

The pattern has always been the same -- from bondage to spiritual faith ... from spiritual faith to great courage ... from courage to liberty ... from liberty to abundance ... from abundance to selfishness ...from selfishness to complacency ... from complacency to apathy ...from apathy to dependency ... and from dependency back to bondage!

Do you truthfully think as individuals and as a nation we're headed back to the bondage from which we came -- with history repeating itself?

No, history doesn't have to repeat itself. That's fiction. That's what the historians say. That's not what the Lord says. A man who follows the Lord doesn't live in a cycle. He doesn't follow the pattern of the world. He follows Christ. His life is changed -- and his life is full and his life is great!

I have taught thee in the way of wisdom; I have led thee in right paths.

Proverbs 4:11

What's exciting?

I put it to you. Which is more thrilling -- to condemn or to salvage a man? Which is more thrilling -- to be drunk, helpless or hopeless -- or by the grace of God, to dry out, become sober and remain sober?

Which is more exciting -- to see lives torn apart or put together? Which is more exciting -- hangovers, creepy men or a clear head, a new day and knowing it's a gift?

Once you become a Christian and see for the very first time the hand of God ... you can understand the tragedy in your own life. You can understand why certain things had to happen in order that you might be blessed. You begin to realize all these acts we see on earth are not just independent and strange. There is a connection -- and God's hand is in everything. That's exciting.

When you realize not one single bird falls from the sky without the Lord knowing it, noting it, and loving it ... and then discover how much more precious a man or woman is, that's exciting.

Look at the birds of the air; they do not sow or reap or store away in barns, and yet your heavenly Father feeds them. Are you not much more valuable than they?

Matthew 6:26

Deals or promises?

Jesus walks right into the eye of the storm of trouble.

Let me help you, He says. It is for times like these that I have loved you. I have made you promises. I told Abraham at age 100, with his wife Sarah 90, that she would bear him a child through whom the entire world would be blessed, and all his descendants.

Dead in the body ... and Abraham knew it, but he believed God.

Why? Because God makes promises -- not deals. **Sarah became pregnant and bore a son to Abraham in his old age, at the very time God had promised him.**

When He makes a promise, He's able to perform it. You and I can make promises from now until breakfast that we will not be able to perform.

Every promise of Scripture is to the man or woman who takes God at His word -- that He has loved you, that His death was for the forgiveness of every sin in your life.

That He intends you good, that He wants you to call upon His strength right in the center of the storm of trouble ... for the rest of your natural life.

Genesis 21:2

Rolling with the tide

If you seek to run with the majority, to go with the tide, or if you seek the fellowship and the companionship of the world ... you can never come to Christ.

Every Christian experiences what it means to stand as a minority of just one, in a tide that is not going your way -- and will never go your way, until Jesus comes again.

Enter ye in at the strait gate: for wide is the gate, and broad is the way, that leadeth to destruction, and many there be which go in thereat: because strait is the gate, and narrow is the way, which leadeth unto life, and few there be that find it.

This narrow way is the way of the man who follows Jesus. Jesus says,
If any man will come after Me, let him deny himself and follow Me.

That leaves a scar. Most scars are in the defense and offense of ego. A man must put aside his ego ... deny it ... pick up his cross ... which will involve many scars ... and follow Christ.

Matthew 7:13
Luke 9:23

Overestimating optimism and pessimism

The whole world loves an optimist because he sees others in action and deed, events, the unfolding of history in the *best* possible light.

Frankly, the whole world hates a *pessimist* because he sees others in word and deed, events, the unfolding of history in the *worst* possible light.

You know what is the major ingredient of pessimism ... ignoring success and dwelling on failure. We see that with our young people, beginning in the 1960's, running down this country ... with everything this country has done wrong or unsuccessfully ... totally forgetting it has done more things right than any other nation that has ever existed on the face of the earth.

But pessimism has become contagious. Now the older generation thinks like the younger generation -- and everyone is *pessimistic.*

Most of our *optimism* is in *overestimating man* and *underestimating God.* Most of our *pessimism* is *underestimating God.*

Would it surprise you to know that neither optimism or pessimism is Biblical?

The gift ...

We only understand grace ...
the gift of God ...
when we realize
that we've come
to know Christ.

He asks that
we use our lives
to tell others ...
to show others

Christ in our lives,
Christ on our lips,
and Christ in our values
and our time.

My grace is sufficient for thee:
for My strength is made perfect in weakness.

II Corinthians 12:9

Values that don't change

We've gotten terribly confused.
Jesus didn't come from heaven to earth
so that you and I might ultimately not go to hell.

Jesus came from heaven to earth so that you and
I might ultimately be the righteousness of God
in Jesus Christ.

The Bible says:
**He who knew no sin was made to be sin itself that
we might be made the righteousness of God in Him.**

> You want happiness?
> Go with the crowd.
> You want the little, fleeting, fluttering things
> that people give their eye tooth for?
> Go with the crowd.

Do you want joy ... do you want meaning ...
do you want purpose ... do you want values that don't
change ... that are absolute now and in eternity?

Then you enter the straight gate, and you follow the
straight Christ ... and it will take you there.

II Corinthians 5:21

Get a life!

It's quiet.
And I'm thinking.
How did I get where I am?
Why did I get where I am?
I'm not the person I want be.
I'm not the person I'm supposed to be.
I've just never been sure.

I think of myself as good person.
But I feel gult -- inside I feel guilt.
And I want to be forgiven.
I've gone with the crowd.
But I feel alone even in a crowd.
If there is a God, inside I'm at war with God;
but I want peace with God.

My faith has been misplaced.
I want a faith that is not misplaced.
I can't forgive myself.
I wonder if Jesus would forgive me.
I'm tired of the past.
I want a future.

Be it known unto you therefore, men and brethren, that through this man is preached unto you the forgiveness of sins.

Acts 13:38

Reaching maturity ...

Paul speaks of maturity ...
reaching maturity in the fullness that Christ offers.

I didn't know that being a Christian was tough.
I didn't dream it was tougher than being a pagan.
It is.

I thought the temptations that I now had, with Christ
defending me, would be less. They've *increased*.

I thought I would automatically understand more
things. As a matter of fact, more things mystified me
because, very frankly, I started looking at things I had
never looked at.

I looked at peer pressure ... and peer pressure today is
the greatest opposition there is to the Christian Church.
And so often, peer pressure is within the Christian
Church. "How do I get it all together?" you wonder.

**Knowing this that our old man was crucified with
Him, that the body of sin might be done away with,
that we should no longer be slaves of sin. For sin
shall not have dominion over you, for you are not
under law but under grace.**

Romans 6:9-14

Absolutely confident

The Bible says no man lives godly in Jesus Christ who will not be persecuted. That's a promise as real as any other promise in Scripture. You follow Jesus Christ … you take risk.

The Bible doesn't really call for optimism or pessimism. No, neither one. It calls for *confidence* … realistic confidence in Jesus Christ.

This is why the Apostle Paul could say:
I am utterly persuaded that neither death nor life nor angels nor principalities nor things present nor things to come is able to separate me from the love of God which is in Christ Jesus the Lord.

You may have given up on yourself. Christ hasn't. You may be horribly pessimistic when you look in the mirror. Christ isn't.

Christ sees in us things we never see in ourselves.

What a Christ!
Never pessimistic.
Never optimistic.
Absolutely confident.

Romans 8:38-39

Exception

We are all inclined to think that the rules
and the regulations -- and the Commandments
and the orders only apply
to the other fellow.

God preaches impartiality,
and anyone who disobeys Him is punished --
whether a believer
or nonbeliever.

Whoever follows Christ
is not a privileged person --
he's a *blessed* person,
but not privileged.

This is hard for so many people to realize.
In other words, there is no guarantee
of immunity from bad health
or suffering.

**How blessed is he whose transgression is forgiven,
whose sin is forgiven.**

**For you make him most blessed forever; you make
him joyful with gladness in your presence.**

Psalm 32:1, 21:6

What's it like to be empty?

What's it like to be *empty*?
The alcoholic thinks to himself,
>"If I could just dry out and get sober and be
>sober, it would be the living end.
>Is it enough just *not* to drink?"

One man says,
>"If I gave up this worst sin of my life, I'd be all
>right. Is that enough?"

Is the *morality* that anyone of us can produce within
his *own* power … what the Lord is seeking?

No. A life has to be *filled* once it's *empty*.
It's not just enough *not* to do the things
you did before.

When I became a Christian, I carried forward
my morality. I knew *nothing* of what Jesus
would do in a given situation.

>"How can that be?" you ask.

Because I was *ignorant* of the Christ
I confessed.

How do we "live" Christ?

What do you mean when you say someone's a *mature Christian?*

Is he like bourbon ... bottled, bound, aged?
Does it depend on how long he has professed Christ?
Or does it have to do with the way he *lives* Christ?

When you wake up and think,
    "I am going to have a real godly day,"
and before noon, it's ungodly -- how do you feel about
your Christian life? Your Christian *commitment?*
Your very future?

I wish all of us came to Christ and all of us came with
instant maturity.

How do you teach an unbroken heart ... brokenness?
How do you teach someone who's always been up ...
what it's like to be down? How do you teach an
independent personality to be totally dependent on
the Lord? It's hard, isn't it?

**I have been crucified with Christ and I no longer live,
but Christ lives in me. The life I now live in the body,
I live by faith in the Son of God, who loved me and
gave himself for me.**

Galatians 2:20

Couldn't handle

I don't know about you, but I feel like a fool
looking back at most of my Christian life,
worrying about things I couldn't handle.
Situations I couldn't correct.
People I didn't know ...
and I needed them.

When all the time I could have said,
> "Lord would you please handle this according
> to your ways, knowing the future like the past,
> having a mind that, in my mind, I could never
> fathom and a plan that is eternal? Would you
> handle this?"

I have lived most of my Christian life
surpassing the riches of God's grace
that were available to me.

Are you rich?
Are you poor?
At the Cross, you can answer that.

**Call to Me and I will answer you,
and I will tell you great and mighty things
which you do not know.**

Jeremiah 33:3

Merciful or tolerant?

In today's market, we hope and we pray that God is
tolerant. God is *never, never* tolerant. He is *merciful.*

What a difference. *Merciful* ... but not *tolerating.*

No believer in Christ has the right to be tolerant
where God is *intolerant.* God is the boss.
We are His servants and His slaves.

Not too many people want to talk about being God's
slave. But every believer is to be God's slave.
He is not to go around self-righteously,
judging anyone else.

That kind of judgment is condemned.

But he is not to condone or to tolerate ...
what God says is *wrong.*

**For this God is our God forever and ever.
He will be our guide even unto death.**

**A man's heart devises his way
but the Lord directs his steps.**

Psalm 48:14
Proverbs 16:9

Looking back ...

Most of my life I spent looking back over my shoulder. Solomon, that God says is the wisest man He ever made, cautions about asking why the former days were better.

Gasoline at 15 cents in Houston, including federal and state tax. Five dollars for a date and a bite to eat. Those were the days.

Really? Were they better? You see, the Bible, if it's telling the truth, spells out the sins of business, the social sins, the sexual sins in my life. And any one of those sins bars me or any other person from the kingdom of God. But the good news is it says, "And such were some of you. But you were washed. You were set aside for God's purpose. You were actually acquitted, found not guilty of all the things you'd done."

You say, "But wait a minute. I could tell you with complete clarity the things I did. Nobody could dispute me. I could pass a lie detector test. You tell me that's washed away?"

That's exactly what I'm telling you. And if it hasn't been washed away, then Jesus is a liar. Because, you see, the Bible says God is faithful and righteous. And once I've confessed my sins, I am forgiven, in the name of Jesus. And I'm cleansed from all that dirt in my life. So no matter how often I look back, it isn't there. Maybe this strikes a chord in your life.

Does God owe you anything or everything?

Does God owe you or me anything?
You bet He does. He says: *You be my child; I'll be your Father. I am your Father. I have all the obligations of a Father to protect you, to provide for you, to look after you, to see that nothing really happens to you.*

Everything that is within My power I will use for you. I owe you that because I am your Father. If you're to be my child, you have the responsibility of being My son or My daughter and being loyal to Me as your Father.

What a change that makes when you're depressed ... when you're broke ... when you've totaled your car. Or when you read the statistics that, from ages 15 to 24, in the past 50 years the suicide rate has tripled. Those with their whole lives before them have snuffed out their lives.

Does God owe you everything, or anything?
He owes you everything a father owes his child, provided you're His child. Are you His son? Are you His daughter? Let me tell you something. He'll honor you ... and love you ... and met your needs ... and never forsake you!

I will be his Father and he will be my son.

I Chronicles 17:13

The difference between knowledge and wisdom

A lot of us today mistake knowledge and wisdom.
Knowledge is information.
Knowledge is whatever information you retain ...
you store up ... your reserve.

It's the computer of the human mind.

But wisdom is acquired.
Wisdom is acquired by taking God
at His word and living that way -- in the faith
that He is *not* a liar
and --in the faith that
He *alone* is God.

**With the Lord one day is like a thousand years
... and a thousand years like one day.**

The Psalmist says,
**A thousand years are like a watch in the night ...
one night.**

Then the Psalmist, speaking of the Lord, says,
**So teach us to number our days, that we may apply
our hearts unto wisdom.**

II Peter 3:8
Psalm 90:4,12

What is the Christian life?

What is the Christian life?
Is it being happy --
and having a good life?
Not according to Scripture.

It doesn't have that kind of ease.
It has never been offered
in that fashion.

And there's no deception to anyone
who will read Scripture -- and
take God's Word.

Wherefore also we pray always for you, that our God would count you worthy of this calling, and fulfill all the good pleasure of his goodness, and the work of faith with power:

That the name of our Lord Jesus Christ may be glorified in you, and ye in him, according to the grace of our God and the Lord Jesus Christ.

II Thessalonians 1:11-12

Playing with words ...

God doesn't play around with words. In the Sermon on the Mount, Jesus explains what He means when He says, **Do not judge so that you will not be judged.**

You see a speck in the other man's eyes, Jesus says. You go over and try to remove the speck from his eye but **First take the log out of your own eye ...** and you're unaware of it.

Does Jesus say anything about not trying to remove the speck? Oh no. He says, **First remove the log from your eye. Then remove the speck from the other brother's eyes.**

What is Jesus talking about?
The criticism, the critical attitude, the critical spirit.

Not just of pagans, but of so many Christians. Always pronouncing judgment on the other man just as though He were God for a day! Or for a week! Or for a lifetime! And Jesus cautions us against it.

Examine yourselves to see whether you are in the faith; test yourselves.

Matthew 7:1-5
II Corinthians 13:5

Who is talking about Jesus?

It has been an exciting week in Jerusalem.
Jesus has come on a colt from Bethany up to
Jerusalem. His Disciples, fresh with a reminder of the
resurrection of Lazarus … are screaming in a festive
mood.

**Blessed is the King who comes in the name of the
Lord! Peace in Heaven and glory to the Highest!**

Nothing is orchestrated. It is really spontaneous. No
balloons going up on cue. Spontaneous exuberance.

The excitement of all the hidden hopes in their lives …
all their anticipation about the future …
all the inward joys that they covet for their lives …
all of it just spills over into that moment, as Jesus
makes what is termed His *triumphant entry* into
Jerusalem.

From the sidelines the Pharisees yell at Jesus,
**Teacher! Caution your Disciples to keep quiet, and
not to yell at you in this fashion.**

If they were to remain silent, Jesus says, glancing up,
the stones would scream.

Luke 19:38-40

An offer you can't refuse

Do you know there's a day coming when Jews are
going to be open to Jesus as so many Gentiles are?

"But," you say, "they rejected the Jesus."

Should any Gentile be presumptuous enough to claim
that God's chosen people are not still His people?

In the book of Romans we're told:
**Who became God's counselor? For from Him, and
through Him, and to Him are all things** ...

It's that simple!
Here's the offer you can't refuse --
a patience that does not run out but is so
fantastic that prophet after prophet was sent
... and then Jesus, God the Son Himself -- and
a mercy so extensive that we who were prisoners
of our own sin have been released and freed
to live Christ ... and to love Him,
whether Jew, whether Gentile!

That's an offer you really can't refuse ... and it's what
the Lord is all about.

Romans 11:34-35

Is Jesus the Messiah?

The Samaritan woman stands at Jacob's well. She listens to her life unfold, standing there with this Jewish stranger. Instantly trying to get him off the subject, she asks him to talk about whether it's proper to worship in Samaria or down in Jerusalem. He says salvation is through the Jews and that Jerusalem is the right place.

Jesus responds, **But let me tell you, neither place matters, because when God comes, He's going to count worship not by the place, but by whether it's in spirit and in truth.**

I know when the Messiah comes, she says. **He'll settle all these things.**

I who speak to you am He, Jesus replies.

You hear so many people say that Jesus never claims that He is The Messiah. Mark this well ... in Chapter 4 of the Gospel of John ... He definitely does claim it.

And her reaction?
She goes off into the town.
There's a man I met.
He told me everything that I've ever done!

John 4:7-29

Anxiety

"Anxiety -- how could that happen to a man of faith?" It happens to you and me. The Lord doesn't have any illusions about either one of us.

Each one of us comes to a time in his or her life when at best we have to cry out --
> "Lord, help thou mine unbelief. I'm so anxious, I'm so hesitant and so indecisive. I'm in such pain. It hurts so much. You've just got to take my word -- I want you to help my unbelief."

That's right -- the Lord reaches out and helps you in your unbelief ... not just your belief. He knows what we're made of. He knows where we're coming from. He knows from having become a man and having walked on this earth -- how hard it is to be a believer and how hard it is to follow a Christ the world denies. He understands.

You insist on understanding all about it? Then you'll never trust Him ... you'll keep your anxieties. But if you recognize that if God could be completely understood by either you or me,
then He wouldn't be God.

Cast all your anxieties upon Him, for He cares for you.

I Peter 5:7

Are you playing with Christ?

Christ changes lives, and if He hasn't changed yours, perhaps it's because you have never asked Him,
"Lord, what would you have me do?"

I thank God that He has given me the ability to be a different man than the man I chose to be -- that He has given different orders than the orders to which I by nature responded.

That He set different values than the values I'd chosen -- all of them within love that I had never seen -- and could scarcely believe.

Are you only playing with words and dabbling with Christ? Or are you willing to take Him at His Word, and say that anyone who would go to Calvary for you has the right to command your life?
"Lord what do you want me to do?
You're not just my Savior ... You're my Lord and from You I will take my orders."

That's the call of Scripture ..."Lord what do you want me to do?" If you've asked, and you have your orders, are you obeying? The Lord Jesus would love to have you deal with Him.

Let your change of heart be seen in your works.

Matthew 3:8

Defining success

What defines a genuine success?

If you are a Christian, I would urge you
to re-examine your failures today
and see if they have not already
proved to be a
spiritual blessing
in your life.

I've known a great many men and women
who have succeeded in their professions
and their businesses --
but who have denied Christ
and will be judged by Him
as failures.

The Scripture tells us ...

**For the foolishness of God is wiser than men,
and the weakness of God is stronger than man.**

**But God has chosen the foolish things in the world
to shame the wise, and God has chosen the weak
things of the world to shame the things which are
strong.**

I Corinthians 1:25-28

Did you duck?

Fred Smith tells the story …

> "I used to travel a lot when I was speaking coast-to-coast. A man sitting next to me on the plane talked to me about business for a couple of hours."

> "Then he turned to me and asked, 'Where is it you're going?'"

> "San Francisco," I said.

> "And you're going there on business?"

> "Yes."

> "And what do you plan to do?"

> "I'm going to speak to a group of businessmen."

> "And what are you going to speak about?"

> "I came to the crossroads," Fred Smith said. "I could have told him motivation. I could have told him about the crises in business. I could've told him how to conquer through cash flow. I hesitated … and then I said … Jesus Christ. I didn't duck."

I will instruct you and teach you in the way you should go.

Psalm 32:8

Stupid or smart?

Jesus calls together his 12 Apostles. I'm going to send you out, He says. I don't want you to take a change of clothing. I don't want you to take sandals, a bag or any form of money. Not even a staff for your protection.

"It must've been a pretty safe world," you say.

No, as a matter of fact, it was a very dangerous world. From secular sources we learn that, in the time of Jesus, if three men were walking at dusk along the road, the prevalent thought of each of the men was this,

"Will I be the one the other two kill?"

Morality had sunk that low. Violence escalated to that point. Imagine telling your 12 Apostles to go out without even a staff for protection in that kind of world, with no money to provide for your needs, with no sandals for your feet -- not even a bag or change of clothing.

"That's pretty naive," you say.

That's right. Jesus was sending them through many towns and they would be gone for weeks. What was He teaching them? *To trust Him* in that kind of world.

Matthew 10:5-14

Atheist?

What is an atheist?
I know. I was one.
If there is no God, I don't have to answer for my
thoughts or my actions.
If there is no God, I'm a free agent. I'm on my own.
If there is no God, the Bible is a lie.
And if there is no God, there's no one I can pray to.

Atheism today is the *in thing*. Eight percent of
Americans claim to be atheist. And on the college
campus, it's the *in thing* to say "I am an atheist."
Great way to rebel against parents -- tell them,
"I'm an atheist." They won't know what to say.
In the Bible, if it's to be believed, the Apostle Paul
makes an amazing statement with a lot of logic. "If
the dead are not raised, if there is no life after death,
then let's eat, and drink, for tomorrow, we die."

If there is no God, then Stalin in the Soviet Union,
Mao Zedong in China, Hirohito in Japan, Hitler in
Germany and Mussolini in Italy -- they all got away
with it. Scot-free. They all killed millions.

But if there is no God, I'm stuck with my guilt and my
past. I'm anxious about the future.
And then I remember if there's nothing in my life
that means everything -- there's nothing in my life
that means anything.

Own it!

How many years I tried to pass the buck.

> "No matter how history judges my
> personal morality, I alone am responsible
> for the dropping of the bomb,"
> Harry S. Truman,
> President of the United States.

He is remembered for his statement,
> "The buck stops here, with me."

What a contrast with the Roman Governor in
Jerusalem who judged Jesus.

He found Jesus innocent. And then, in front of a
public mob, he washed his hands of any responsibility
for His blood and turned right around and decreed Jesus
was to be crucified.
> "Not my fault. I found him innocent.
> Not my decision. I washed my hands.
> But crucify him."

I know how many times I tried to pass the buck --
blaming God. Blaming circumstances.
Bringing up all the ifs, ands and buts --
but never taking responsibility
for my own life.

Abundant life

When a company recruits you, it promises happiness. When you fall in love, you seek happiness. As you put a little money aside, you try to ensure happiness.

With everyone's plans for happiness, why are so many people miserable?

Christians are not immune from afflictions.
The Bible says,
Many are the afflictions of the righteous.

If the abundant life involved good health, you would never find an afflicted Christian. If the abundant life assured you would have total peace at home, you would never have a rebellious child. If the abundant life meant being rich, you would never find a poverty-stricken Christian.

But you see, *abundant life* is something far above the super abundance that is in the person of Jesus Christ.

The abundant life is forever. It isn't dependent on other things or knowing what tomorrow holds.

Psalm 34:19

Jesus is my friend

When you hear something at least a hundred times from your father, you're likely to remember it. When I was nine years old, my father said, "Ben, if you have two real friends in your life, you will have one more than the average man has to show for his life."

How do you choose a closest friend?
Well, I would choose him for illness, for reversals, for failure, for sorrow -- for death. I'd be realistic about it.

Bob McClure was more like a child than any grown man I've ever known. He showed no pretense, no put-on at all. He was an executive with a national trucking firm operating out of Miami. He was on his deathbed -- at 37. Two sons, one daughter, a beautiful wife. And he looked at me, and he said, "It's all right. Jesus is my friend."

The Bible says a friend loves at all times, under any circumstances. The Bible says, **Wealth adds many friends.** The Bible says that **the man of many friends comes to ruin.** Why? Because they're not real. And then I discovered that Jesus loves me. He says, **I will never forsake you. I will stick closer to you than a brother. I will be with you in time and in eternity.**

I said, "Man, that's the kind of friend I want." But all of that friendship starts at the Cross. That's why I can understand Bob McClure saying,

"It's all right. Jesus is my friend."

Is faith something you do?

If you know Christ --
what are the benefits of Christ?
Is He worth it?

Moses said so -- and men and women of God
throughout the ages
have thought so.

Faith is not something
you just have.
Faith is something you do
with your life.

**So faith comes from hearing,
and hearing by the Word of Christ.**

**Bear one another's burdens, and so fulfill
the law of Christ.**

**So then as we have opportunity, let us do good to
everyone, and especially to those who are of the
household of faith.**

Romans 10:17
Galatians 6:2-10

Is it possible to have new spiritual energy?

> "Ben, it holds such sorrow for me to look back
> and think of all the things I've *blown* in my life."

The Lord does not deal with what we have blown in
our lives ... except to *forgive*. He deals with the love
of Christ.

> "How can I matter this much?"

It is all explained in this simple statement:
you can **cast all your anxieties upon Him** ...
and you're invited to do it ...
because He cares for you.

May I suggest that you not live any New Year expecting
to change ... but that you live the New Year as the
beginning of your *eternal life*.

When you take the measure of your actions, realize:
> Would I do this in the presence of
> Jesus Christ?
> Would I take Him where I'm going?

**Humble yourselves therefore, under the mighty
hand of God that He may exalt you in the proper
time, casting all your anxieties upon Him, because
He cares for you.**

I Peter 5:6-7

When you crash

Everyone sees it in the Prodigal Son.
That magic phrase: **He came to his senses.**
Meaning what? Meaning ... he had crashed, his life
was in shambles, and he had his own re-examination.
> "Oh," you say, "he studied himself -- how rotten
> he was, how he'd thrown everything away on
> wine, women and song."

Yes, there was some of that. But do you know what
he primarily re-examined? His father -- the kind of
person he was, the kind of love he had, the kind of
compassion he extended, the kind of forgiveness he
practiced.
> "I'm dying of hunger," he says. "There are
> people who work for my father who have
> more than enough to eat. I know I'm not
> worthy to be his son -- but I am going to go
> to him and throw myself on his mercy and
> ask just to be a hired man."

He may not have known himself, but he knew his father.
Long before he saw his father, his father saw him! He
didn't stand on ceremony. He didn't wait for any
speeches. His father ran to him, threw himself on his
son, kissed him, and embraced him. That re-examination
had saved the life of the Prodigal Son.

Luke 15:11-32

Our first attraction ...

You see, when we are first attracted to Christ, all we hear is sin and the forgiveness of sin, and that is the Good News.

That is the Gospel. That is what counts.

But when you spell out the daily following of Christ --
when you spell out that every believer is to take Christ's physical place on earth ...
not silently, not inactively, not impersonally ...
but right up there in the marketplace --
involved in other people's lives! Boy, that's hard!

We were built for life, not for death.
We were built for eternity, not time.
We were built for Christ and for each other.
Yes, in every church and in synagogues throughout
the world, when the words of Jesus are examined, many
find it very difficult to believe, and want no part of it.

But, those who stick to His Word under the most severe circumstances find their faith increasing ... and find their love for Him increasing -- and His love for them increasing.

O love the Lord, all ye His saints, for the Lord preserves the faithful and plentifully rewards the proud doer.

Psalm 31:23

Elevating your faith

Do I have to become a dumb-dumb, a little stupid …
to follow a Christ you cannot see, in a fashion the
world simply doesn't understand. What is the part
your mind has in the eyes of Almighty God?

Jesus in his public ministry had a man who asked:
**Teacher, what is the greatest commandment in the
law?**

**You shall love the Lord God with all your heart,
with all your soul, and with all your mind.**

Jesus replied.

In other words, the great commandment to you and
me, is to love the Lord our God with all our mind.

That kind of elevates it, doesn't it?

**The things you have learned and received and heard
and seen in me, practice these things; and the God
of peace shall be with you.**

Matthew 22:36-37
Philippians 4:9

Like a child

Do we all come to Christ on different levels,
determined by wealth, education or society?
There's one level and *only one!*
The Bible says,
**Except you be converted and become as little
children, you cannot enter into the Kingdom of God.**

Well how do you become as *little children*?
You have a child mind, hanging on to everything you
hear -- ready to learn, ready to follow and ready to
imitate. You have a child's heart. You trust God.

When He says,
> *I'll catch you!*
He means it and you assume that's correct.
He'll catch you.

You don't come up with the arguments or the
controversies or the re-examination of all ... the
analytical approach.

Just like a child. A child's love ... you love a child,
he'll love you back. A child has a sensitivity of love
that so often adults do not have, because so many of
us hide our hearts behind our brains.

Matthew 18:3
Luke 18:17

Who is the role model?

I remember John D. Rockefeller in American history. He was one of the most despised citizens of this nation until a Public Relations man went to him and said,
> "Give away some money. It will make you a hero."

Rockefeller did -- and died a hero.

Who is your role model?
If it is a believer in Christ … have you been disappointed in that woman or that man?
Is that the crowd you want to run with?

Even though you greatly admired the person and respected him and looked at everything he did throughout your life, were you not eventually disillusioned in that role model without exception?

Has anyone ever been disappointed in Jesus Christ as his role model?
I never have.

Make sure that your character is free from the love of money; being content with what you have; for He Himself has said, I will never desert you nor will I ever forsake you.

Hebrews 13:5

What you cannot repay

I want to ask you today -- in your own life,
does it repel you -- what Christ has done for you --
that you cannot repay? What you cannot afford?
What you cannot work out?

Does it offend you that the worst people you know
are more open to Christ than the best people you
know? Why? Because we are all caught up in pride as
though we have something to offer God -- unaware
that we have nothing to offer God.

God offers us Christ with eternal forgiveness and
eternal life -- and His promises are good throughout
the world. God's power is real.

God has promised to meet every need of the believer
on the face of the earth -- that means in chaos, in
recession, in death, in health, in separation and
alienation. And He has never lied.

Now you can understand why the very best people
you know so often want nothing to do with Christ ...
because it is humiliating at the foot of the Cross.

**And my God will meet all your needs according to
the riches of his glory in Christ Jesus.**

Philippians 4:19

He knows

Your heart never breaks without God knowing it.
If He knows a thought before it's formed in your mind,
why would He not know when your heart is broken?

I don't care what the need is in your life or mine ...
the Lord deals with us as an only child.

When you have an only child ... that's special. You're
interested in your child's every action ... every thought
... every line of reasoning.

Can you imagine just revealing to one woman at the
well, the Samaritan who would have been locally known
as the prostitute ... the woman that had no one to
associate with her during the daytime ... can you
imagine the Lord being so interested in her that He
revealed everything she had done ... *and He still loved
her?*

Most of us in the dark side of our lives hope that the
Lord doesn't know. He does. And the bright side of
our lives? He does.

As a Heavenly Father, He evaluates it ... but love
overrules.

**Come see a man who told me all the things that I
ever did: is this not the Christ?**

John 4:29

Friendship

"What is a friend?" you ask.

In every man there's a man and a little boy.
When the man in me likes the man in you,
we're just *acquaintances.*

When the man and the little boy in me likes
the man and the little boy in you,
we're *friends*.

> "Is this a friendship that I can arbitrarily
> choose?" you ask. "A friendship with Jesus
> Christ?"

Not at all.

I choose my own friends, Jesus Christ points out.
You did not choose me; I chose you.

It's a one-sided friendship ... but oh,
what a wonderful friendship!

**These things I have spoken to you, that my joy
may be in you, and that your joy may be full.**

John 15:11,16

How serious is my sin?

If you tell me your view of sin,
I can tell you your view of punishment.

We take punishment lightly because we take sin
lightly.

But how seriously does God take punishment?

So seriously that when Jesus bore my sin and
He went to the Cross and endured my hell for my sin ...
that personal and that agonizing.

That's the measure of punishment
that God sees necessary for sin.

There are a lot of things I've done that I wouldn't
have done -- if I'd known I was doing it against the
living Lord.

I would have done a double take on most of my life.
I would've wondered -- how did I miss it?

**And these shall go away into everlasting
punishment: but the righteous into life eternal.**

Matthew 25:46

Greed or God?

Who caused the financial crisis?
Wall Street or Main Street?
Or was it Congress?
Or was it a guy like me -- wanting a home
that he couldn't afford but he wanted to flip it and
make a profit.

Is the financial crisis the result simply of greed?
Or is it the result of God?
Did you notice when it happened automatically
Americans looked to the government --
and not to God?

But the Bible says, **I the Lord make well-being.
I cause calamity. I the Lord do all these things**.

Is the object of the financial crisis to get our attention
and to remind us that our roots are in the living Lord --
and how far we've gotten away from it?

Do we depend upon the Lord or do we depend upon
the government? Do we actually think Congress is in
control or the Lord is in control?

I believe the Lord is in control. And I want to learn
from this crisis. And like every other American, it has
cost me and has probably cost you. Not my life, not
my confidence, not my faith.

Isaiah 45:7

The conditions of our world include ...

We like to pretend that times have changed.
They haven't. We all like to pretend that the problems
have changed. They haven't. Walter Cronkite, a
television news anchor over 30 years ago, was asked
to name the number one problem in the world.

> "Well, I would have to answer it in this
> fashion," he said.

> "First of all, population. Second pollution.
> Third, depletion of natural resources
> including food. Fourth, atomic full
> information. If we don't get a handle on
> atomic proliferation, the civilization will not
> survive."

A new set of problems occupies our news headlines
today. But God says there is one problem --
the sin in my life *that alienates* me from God.

**I have told you these things, so that in me you
may have peace. In this world you will have trouble.
But take heart!
I have overcome the world.**

John 16:33

Tithing

There's a Federal judge who heard a case of a couple in New Hope, Minnesota who had routinely tithed. They had given 10% off the top of their gross income to their Church. In one year they tithed ... $13,450. The next year they filed for bankruptcy.

The US District Court held that since this couple received no value for their donation to their Church the year before ... it constituted a fraudulent transfer of funds. The court called upon the Church to give back to the *court* -- the $13,450 given the year before by this couple.

No value! If this couple had bought lottery tickets, it would've been legal. That would have been considered value. Refrigerator. Car. Vacation.

Whatever else it might have been ... it wouldn't have constituted a fraudulent transfer of funds, according to this court. But they received *nothing of value* for their tithe to the Church.

How far we have come ... that we discount the obedience of believers who choose to worship together and underwrite with love and resources ... the worship of Christ and advancing the kingdom of God.

Overcoming the back slide

We sing:
> "*I need thee every hour*" ... and oh, that's true.

Today in your own life you may be calloused, whereas you were once warm toward the things of the Lord. You may have once believed the Bible. Now you don't.

You may have made an effort to follow Christ. Now you don't and you're wondering:
> "Am I a person who has looked back once
> I had put my hand to the plow ...
> and am not worthy of the kingdom?
> I've never been worthy of the kingdom."

The Lord said:
Hosea you tell them, return to me; I will freely forgive them. I'll be like that dew to the people of Israel. You tell them I'm that same God.
> "How can we be sure?" you ask.

Because Jesus forgave Peter. And Peter went on from there ... following Christ and honoring Him. According to tradition, eventually Peter lost his life just for claiming the name of Jesus.

Once a coward ... then a hero. Once unbalanced, then balanced. Once inconsistent, then consistent. That's the story of all of us.

Hosea 14:1-7

Problem ... solution

There's an old saying and it's very popular:
"If you have no solutions, you have no problems."

Now that's very charming if you think about it.
You can shrug off just about anything
that comes along --
but it happens to be a lie.

We have the problem, and it has never changed with
any generation or any civilization ...
sin that alienates us from God

and we have an answer -- God's answer:
Reconciliation to that God in Jesus Christ His only Son.

Now you might think you can add to that.
You can't.
"Should I believe that because you say so?"

Obviously not. But my heart tells me that it's true.
I have every confidence your heart tells you that it's
true. Don't argue with your heart ... your heart's right.

**Everyone who calls on the name of the Lord
will be saved.**

Romans 10:13

Worried about tomorrow?

I am anxious about tomorrow.
You're anxious about tomorrow.

The most natural thing in the world is to be
anxious about tomorrow.

After all, tomorrow is one of the most
anxious days we've ever faced.

If you don't believe it,
wait until it's dark to think about it.

Anxious about tomorrow ...
the most natural thing in the world.

Yet the Lord cautions us against it.

Why?

**Do not be anxious about anything, but in
everything, by prayer and petition, with
thanksgiving, present your requests to God.**

Philippians 4:6

Rejoicing with a balanced life!

I have seen people who have *rejoiced* ... as they understand rejoicing ... and let their families go to pot.
Tell me how you rejoice in cancer. I've never known
anyone who has rejoiced in cancer, who had his right
mind ... in losing your business or having your home
burned down ... in being alienated from your children
or your spouse. Not reasons for rejoicing.

But no matter what people problem you have ... no
matter what situation you find yourself in ... no matter
what confronts you... Paul's advice is -- *don't rejoice
always because of those things ... but rejoice in the Lord,
because He hasn't changed and He loves you. No
matter what, rejoice in the Lord.*

Not rejoice always, the way it is so often told. That
makes you look like a nut. It makes you act like a nut.
The Lord doesn't say that. *The reason for rejoicing is
that you're in the Lord.* How does that work?

As a believer, you're in Christ. Christ is in you. That's
the relationship. It is eternal. Nothing human can
destroy it. It is a gift of God and it's the reason, no
matter what the situation ... to rejoice.

Rejoice in the Lord always. Again I will say, rejoice!

Philippians 4:4

Patience

Then we come to the patience of Christ --
who sees on every hand the denial of His love.

In the wisdom of God, He must wonder:

What more could I have done for you
than I promised to do ...
and then that I did do?
What point did I overlook?
What facet of myself did I not make clear?
What is it about me that you find unbelievable ...
my innocence or my guilt ...
because of your sins?

Do you think that the Cross was theatrical ...
or do you think it was essential?
Do you think it was a high point in history
or the low point of history?

Do you think it was for you ...
or for everyone else?

How He loves me ... how imperfect I am.
How compassionate is my Christ.
Blessed be the name of a patient Christ ...
with an impatient people!

Born of God

Have you ever stopped to think of those who are not believers in Jesus Christ, but who live more like believers than the ones who are? I've seen men 75 years old dying. When I ask,

> "What do you believe about Jesus?"

They'll say,

> "Oh, I'm a Christian. I think I was 20 … 21.
> I went forward in a Church."

> "Have you had much to do with Jesus since then?" I'll ask.

> "No. Not much.
> Not much. But I'm a Christian."

Rather than listening to what man says -- listen to what God says.

We have built up a nation in which the Christian Church demands only profession … not performance. But that is absolutely contrary to God's Word.

The Lord says,

Whoever is born of God born from above, born again … cannot continue the pattern of sin in his life, because a seed of God remains in him.

That's a promise in the statement.

I John 5:18-20

Shrinking from the future?

The glory of the Lord is that He has revealed the divine
future of every man who trusts Jesus. Who has said:
**The day is coming when every tear will be wiped
away,** *when all sorrow will be removed, when there will
not be any pain, however severe it is today, and when
there will be no death.*

That's a divine future, which is fully revealed in Jesus
Christ. When God the Son became flesh, He didn't lose
the power to know the future, the future of His own
flesh as well as the divine future. Do you recall that in
the flesh, even Jesus shrank from knowing the future?

In the Garden of Gethsemane -- when He knew what
was coming up -- He was the only person to
experience hell who knew what it was like
before He experienced it.
That's Jesus and He shrank from it.
Yet knowing that future, He did not shrink from living
it -- and from enduring it.

If I'd only known. If I'd only known.
Thank God ... we don't ...
but thank God we know all we need to know,
revealed in Christ and proven as we live Him.

Isaiah 25:8

Do you belong to Christ?

If you were to die tonight, what would your friends say? What would you say in the presence of Almighty God when He asks you this question,
>   "Do you belong to Christ?"

Think of your lifelong friends who would speculate on whether or not you are a Christian. They've known you for many years. They know your politics. Your wives had been pregnant at the same time. You've almost had fistfights. You've played golf or bridge together and you've even argued over your scores and bids. If you were to die, about all they can say is,
>   "Well, he's belonged to the Church
>   down the street for some years."

That's all they can base their judgment on.

The Scriptures tell us that the only person who belongs to Christ ... is the person who has received into his life Jesus Christ as his Savior and his Lord.

Receiving Him as Savior means more than simply believing in Christ ... It means that you trust Him. How many people today could truthfully say,
>   "I believe in Christ, but I do not trust Him?"

He saved us not on the basis of deeds but according to His mercy, by the washing and regeneration and renewing by the Holy Spirit.

Titus 3:5

Short-term or long-term?

My broker said, "I think that stock is a terrific investment long-term." What is long-term? Six months. "Short-term, I think it is lousy." What is short-term? Thirty days. And that pretty much describes the mindset of the average American.

Lane Adams was a friend of mine ... he used to be a nightclub singer in Vegas. He had a voice like Robert Goulet and looked like a Greek God. One of Lane's favorite pastimes was to get on a plane and to call the stewardess back and say, "What are your plans?"

And she said, "Well, after this, I plan to go back to college, and after that, I would hope to be married. And after that, I sure would hope we'd have children. And after that, I hope we'll buy a home. And after that, maybe buy a boat! And after that, I guess we'd retire. And after that, I guess we die!"

"And after that?" Lane would ask. And she'd always pull a blank.

We are not used to thinking beyond short-term. The whole world thinks short-term. But Jesus always thinks long-term. The world thinks of time. Jesus thinks of eternity. He sells a different future. The world sells a different present.

Short-term or long-term?

Voices?

Hearing voices? First thing I'd do is check in with a shrink. That would spook me. A man was walking through SoHo in NYC, between Greenwich Village and Wall Street. And he heard a woman whispering inside his ear. "Who's that?" "Who's there?" "It is not your imagination."

Can you think of anything more intimate, more personal? Naturally he looked around to see the woman. No woman near him. He looked at the other people to see if they heard it ... no indication they did. He was spooked. And he wondered, "Where on earth did that come from? I could hear the words plainly."

Then he looked across the street at a massive billboard advertising a new series on A&E, "Paranormal State" -- about ghosts. Now his curiosity was up. He made his way up to the roof, finding the answer -- a new technology called audio spotlight where you can single out one or more people in a crowd and talk literally inside their ears in a whisper. Now that technology is already being used in museums and in libraries where you want silence, yet you want to talk.

And I began to think, what about the Bible, if it's true. Did other people hear voices throughout history? And I discovered God spoke directly to Adam. He called Abraham, a pagan, out of his people to follow him and he said, **I'm going to take you someplace** but he didn't tell him where. But Abraham followed the voice. And then I found out that God spoke to Solomon in a dream. Then I found out God spoke from heaven to the public about the identity of Jesus as His son. Then I discovered the Bible says no one can call Jesus -- Lord -- except by the Holy Spirit. The Holy Spirit has to speak to you, not from the outside like a loud speaker, but on the inside like the woman whispering in that man's ear.

You say, "Well, that really sounds scientific." Yeah, and I've got a lot of confidence in science, really. Do you have a lot of confidence in yourself? I sure used to. Until I found in the Bible that the man who puts his trust in himself is a fool. And that the wisdom of man, which includes ALL the intellectuals, the education, the ideas, the speculations that we kick around -- the wisdom of man is foolishness to God because the foolishness of God is greater than the wisdom of man.

And it took me back to the day I heard a voice, "Jesus loves me." And, staring straight ahead, unsure I moved my lips, I responded, "I've hated you, but you loved me. I didn't think you existed but you can talk to me and I can hear you. Lord Jesus, you want me? You got me." I did hear his voice. And with this new technology, if I had the ability to whisper into the ear of everyone on the face of the earth, I would use only three words. *Jesus Loves You.*

The object of Scripture

It's an amazing thing that
in this life we forget what really is
the object of Scripture.

That over and above teaching ...
over and above bringing us under the conviction
that we're wrong ...
over and above being the plumb line
to judge all the ideas
that come down the pike ...

the ultimate idea of Scripture is
to equip us -- as men of Satan ...
to be men of God.
As men of sin ...
to be men of righteousness.
As men and women whose lives count for nothing ...
to count for something!

**All scripture is inspired by God and profitable for
teaching, for reproof, for correction, for training in
righteousness; that the man of God may be
adequate, equipped for every good work.**

II Timothy 3:16-17

How do you tell a Christian?

Today it's difficult to tell who the Christians are because most Christians give Jesus Christ a lot of lip and very little life -- and because they want to remain under their own command rather than let Christ be the commander-in-chief of their lives.

They want to let the change take place outside rather than inside.

All of us have a tendency to walk the broad path which leads to destruction -- and keep one foot on their own path that leads to life.
        The Lord says it cannot be done.

The Lord has never blessed me when I just talked grace and the forgiveness of sins -- because consciously or unconsciously, I have been lying when I've done it.
The Lord never said,
        I want all your lips.
 He taught -- *I want all your lives.*

Repentance is a willingness to live a changed life for Christ.

The time is fulfilled, and the Kingdom of God is at hand; repent and believe in the Gospel.

Mark 1:15

The standard for forgiveness is …

Can you imagine a man of God teaching in a devotional book that forgiveness hinges on sorrow, and repentance, and the confession of the person you forgive?

Don't you know from living, if that were the case … you would forgive practically no one in the course of a lifetime? That's not the standard of Scripture.

The standard of Scripture for the believer in Jesus Christ is that we are to forgive as Christ has forgiven us.

Now that's a standard:
> not whether somebody says he's sorry …
> not whether he deserves it …
> not whether he is innocent …
> not whether he starts living a repentant life.

We are to forgive by the standard by which we have been forgiven. It has nothing to do with the other person.

For if you forgive others for their transgressions, your Heavenly Father will also forgive you.

Matthew 6:14

Whom do you trust?

I'm reminded of what a woman told me when I asked her,

> "Who are you trusting for your salvation?"

> "I tried to keep the Ten Commandments," she replied, "and the Golden Rule. I've always been active in Church and always given generously. You'd be surprised how many committees I've served on, and how many dinners I've fixed."

Her mother has cancer and has been rejected by men, but she could trust her mother to the Lord. Her son is in Germany and she cannot afford to visit him, but she can trust him to the Lord.

But for her own salvation, she trusts her keeping of the Ten Commandments and the Golden Rule, her dinners, her committees, her giving and her Church membership.   No mention of Jesus Christ.

My friend, it is only the blood of Jesus Christ that can blot out your sins. The blood can remove the barrier between you and God. You cannot do this yourself.

**Because of the works of the law
no flesh will be justified in His sight;
for through the law comes knowledge of sin.**

Romans 3:20-21

Stubborness

What are you stubborn about?
Are you stubborn about your faith in Jesus Christ?
No matter what the world says? Or are you just
strangely silent, when people dispute God's plan of
salvation? Are you stubborn about Scripture?

Do you back off whenever someone says,
> "You don't believe it literally, do you?"

> "No, no, who would believe the resurrection
> literally?

> "You don't believe He was really dead on the
> Cross?"

> "Of course not: it was all figurative."

Each time it's hard to believe, someone wants to say:
> "You mean figuratively, not literally?"

God means literally;
otherwise, we are without hope
and He is still stubborn about it.
Are you stubborn about God's Word being God's Word?
About God's promises being God's promises?

**Be still, and know that I am God. I will be exalted
among the nations, I will be exalted in the earth!**

Psalm 46:10

Spiritual alzheimer's ...?

Alzheimer's disease fascinates us today. Forty years ago people had never seen the word ... though it had been identified by Dr. Alzheimer. As you know, it involves a lack of memory, a deterioration of the mind, the incapacity to remember. Some time ago I had a dear friend call me on the phone.

> "I want you to go by and see my mother. She's right at the razor's edge. I think I should mention that to you."

> "Do you remember me?" I asked as I walked in.

> "Of course I remember you," she said.

She chatted on and she obviously did remember. I asked, "What about Frank?" her son. "Has Frank been here today?"

> "Who's Frank?" she said.

She remembered me but not her own son who has been wonderful to her through the years. Most of us are afflicted with spiritual Alzheimer's disease. We will accept anything at the hands of the Lord, and then promptly forget where it came from, that we didn't earn it ... didn't deserve it ... but we got it. Once we've gotten what we want, we forget the Giver.

... then your heart will become proud and you will forget the Lord your God who brought you out ...

Deuteronomy 8:10-14

Dissatisfied?

It's a wonderful thing to be dissatisfied. I was dissatisfied with myself before I came to Christ. I have been dissatisfied with myself since coming to Christ. Why? Because of the contrast. I believed He'd done for me what He said He did ... and I had all those resolutions about what I would do for Him ... and I haven't done them.

I see people on the brink of eternity every day, and yet I find myself often seeing things in terms of time rather than eternity ... and I'm dissatisfied with that. But I'll tell you this: the more dissatisfied I am with myself, the more satisfied I am with Christ. The more I am disillusioned and disappointed and disenchanted and dissatisfied with everything about this life ... this nation ... or this person -- I then am much more satisfied with Christ.

Christ never created man, woman or child to be satisfied with this earth ... with the frailties of this flesh, with the mixed motives that are in every one of us -- but to be satisfied with *Him*.

If anyone is thirsty, let him come to Me and drink. If any man thirst let him come after Me.

If any man be consciously dissatisfied, if any man has a vacuum in his life, let him come to Me.

John 7:37

Is God hands-on or hands-off?

If you've ever been *involved*,
it is traumatic.

You come to a woman ... an alcoholic ... a drug abuser
... with her family. You come with her closest friends.
You come with her employer. You seek, as individuals
and as a group, to intervene in her life.

If you have ever been part of an intervention,
you know the drama of the moment.
You know the cursing and the ridicule.

You know how hard it is to confront
someone you love --
and tell her that her life is useless,
and that she has thrown aside every responsibility
because she is an addict.

Does God intervene?
Does He take a different measure
every time He sees you?
Or does He accept the first measure?

**It does not, therefore, depend on human desire or
effort, but on God's mercy.**

Romans 9:16

Solving problems

Jesus Christ said,
**I've come to solve the problems
in your life.**

You mean in some lives?

No ...
in every life ...
the sin problem.

Jesus hasn't come
to judge you.

He's come
to *forgive* you.

He came to do
what otherwise
you'd have to do
for yourself.

He paid the sin price --
and therefore,
bought you and me.

Do you matter?

Each one of us is unique.
There has never been
anyone like you.
There will never be
anyone like you.
Your opportunities are unique ...
they are not common.
Many of your opportunities are peculiar --
only to you.

When you sometimes wonder in this world,
with all of its overwhelming hatreds and
numbers and masses and movements
... *do I really matter?*

You are essential to Jesus Christ
who has entrusted to you, the believer,
 if you are one,
His love ... His Gospel ...
His strategy for the entire world.

Yesterday, He loved you.
Today, He loves you.
Tomorrow, He will love you.
Nothing will change.

Hebrews 13:8

If I were writing the Bible ...

If I were writing a Bible,
(and perhaps you would do the same thing)
I would speak of those that
have a lot on the ball,
those that accomplish the most
and I would reward them ...
all the things that play *up* to the ego.

Recognition, applause, money,
central figure ...
you know.
Yeah, but that's *not* the way
God plays it *up.*

In God's Word we are told to be humble.
Humble before God and humble before man.

That means the object of life is not ... dog eat dog.
It is not what comes out on *top.*
The object of life is to serve others
in the name and for the glory of Jesus Christ.

**Humble yourself in the presence of the Lord,
and He will exalt you.**

James 4:10

The shepherd's impact

When shepherds were out in the field, they would
make a little compound. Then across the opening, the
shepherd would sleep. You've heard the expression ...
           "Over my dead body."

I think this is where it came from. If anyone got into
the sheep, it was over the dead body of the faithful
Shepherd.

Jesus points out:
the hireling ... the one to whom the owner
delegated shepherding ... he will flee.

He looks out for himself, not the sheep.
But the owner of the sheep -- he lays down his life for
the sheep so they **can go in and come out,** which was
a Jewish expression meaning *safety* and *security* -- to
go in and come out.

Jesus looks and says, in the most positive fashion:
**I am the shepherd. The good Shepherd. Anyone
who comes into the sheepfold except by the door
is a thief and a robber. I am the door.**

John 10:1-9

Peer pressure over 45?

You know, today we put down so many of our young people because they give into peer pressure. In thinking about pressure ... I have never been without peer pressure. Peer pressure is not just found among teenagers. It is found among those under 45, those over 45, and it's found all our lives. There is pressure to *conform* and to think as others do ... to act as others do ... to put their values where others put it ... and that has always been the tendency.

Is a changed life more exciting than a worldly life?
You know it's exciting to me to realize the world, the lust of the flesh, the lust of the eyes and boastful pride of life -- which God tells us about -- is in the process of passing away.

Anyone who stakes his life in the ways of this world has staked his life on a *loser*. Anyone who follows Jesus Christ is always following a *winner* and he's never lost. Do you know what God says?

I have made His name above every name so that at the name of Jesus every knee shall bow. Every tongue shall proclaim ... no one will be tongue-tied no matter what their background or their religion, or anything of that nature ... they will proclaim Him **King of Kings, Lord of Lords.**

Romans 14:11

Believing the Bible

> "Ben I'd give anything in the world
> if I could believe the Bible."

My friend you can.
No matter who tries to tamper with the
Christian faith ... I look for two things:

> (1) Who do they say Jesus is?
> (2) What do they say happened on
> the Cross when Jesus was crucified?

Do their answers hinge on the Bible --
or other sources?

Jesus is the only Son of God.
Jesus said,
If you have seen Me, you have seen the Father.
If you have known Me, you have known the Father.
I and the Father are one.

> "I don't understand that," you say.

God's ways are not our ways.
Neither you nor I can understand
God's ways and -- on the face of it,
these claims defy logic.

John 14:7

Speculating about the future ...

We read in the Gospel of Matthew, Chapter 17, that Jesus takes three Apostles with Him up into a mountain. Suddenly in the most provocative of all His actions, Jesus joined two other men ... dead men ... conversing ... identifiable ... very much alive!

Now James and John and Peter knew it wasn't a theory ... it wasn't just what the Psalmist wrote, it wasn't just what their hearts yearned for ... it was true! The veil of the future was pulled back and they saw the dead men alive. They saw they were identifiable. They saw they could converse. They saw that Jesus was part of that future -- whom He could join and then step back from -- and rejoin the present.

Never again would they be the same. Never again would they speculate about the future because they had seen it. Yet even as they came down the mountain ... having heard the voice of God the Father confirm the person of God the Son, and having seen Elijah and Moses, heroes of their faith, they were sworn to secrecy: **Don't discuss this until I have been raised again from the dead.**

What about the future? Don't you wish you knew it? Aren't you glad you don't?

Matthew 17:9

Is that faith?

What is faith? Faith, to be defined, has to be defined by the behavior of the individual … not by some theory … not by some emotion … not by some settlement … but by the individual's behavior.

The man wrote,
> "I believe in Jesus, 100%. I believe
> He is God in the flesh. I believe He was
> crucified for my sin. I believe He rose
> in the flesh. And I believe He is returning."

> "But, I don't love Jesus and when it comes
> to making choices, I choose my old sin …
> and my old life over my new Lord and
> my new Savior and my new friend …
> Jesus Christ."

That is why George Gallup says less than 12% of confessing Christians in the United States make any serious effort to follow Christ.

That is despite 85% of all Americans claiming that they pray every day.

Now faith is your assurance of things hoped for, the conviction of things not seen.

Hebrews 11:1

The environmentalist

We all can claim to be environmentalists today. We are more concerned with the caribou in the Artic Circle then we are with the billions of barrels of oil potentially needed by this nation. Jesus Christ is an environmentalist, but the only environment that counts in my life and yours is inside us -- and that's where He works. He never said:

> Let me come and live around you ...
> Let me come and be an influence in your life ...
> Let me come and create an environment in which you will realize your potential.

No. He says, *open the door to your life and let Me come into you, and create an environment inside that will bless you there and bless the earth in which you live as my servant, as someone who knows Me, as someone who appreciates Me, as someone who can always live with an expectancy for something more.*

It would be so easy to blame God rather than to say:

> "Jesus this is where you placed me. But because of You, I know there's so much more. *My confidence is in the future.* That's why I'm not dwelling on the past."

The potential of man? It is absolutely magnificent.
Psalm 8

Need a second chance?

Is there really a second chance?
And is it in this life -- or after this life?

One of the top magazines featured an article on the word " if " ... all the speculation of man about his own life. I read it with fascination. If I hadn't blown that opportunity ... if I weren't married ... if there weren't children ... if I didn't have a mortgage I couldn't handle ... if I had just chosen a different career ... if I had started out a lot younger -- if -- if there's such a thing as a second chance.

And then, believe it or not, I found the other name for Jesus is second chance. It's at the Cross that the past is washed away ... that we're forgiven ...that a whole new life becomes available with opportunities we never dreamed of. That's what I found.

So it wasn't really shocking to me when the man came and pleaded with God, "I've committed adultery. I've committed murder. I've made you, God, the laughing stock of the entire nation. Is there such a thing as a second chance for me?"

His name was David. He was the King of Israel, and God had put him on the throne. And believe it or not, God described that same man as -- a man after My own heart. He gave him a second chance. He gave me a second chance.

Why wallow in the past?

I used to be so disappointed in God,
after I became a believer.
I would pray --
and nothing happened.

I would read His Word --
and nothing happened.
I would speculate --
and nothing happened.
In my secret heart,
I used to blame God.

Disappointment is based on your hopes,
your expectations and your anticipation.
And I was disappointed in God.

But as I grew in some knowledge of Him,
I came to realize it was not He who had
disappointed me, but I had disappointed myself.
That was a whole new dimension for me.

Why wallow in the past
when you can have the future?

**And let us not grow weary of doing good, for in
due season we will reap, if we do not give up.**

Galatians 6:9-10

Making God laugh ...

Eloise Litz
is noted
for good talks
and for --
good questions.

> "Do you know how
> to make God laugh?"
> she asked.

> "No."

> "Tell him --
> all your plans."

**The steps of a good man ordered by the Lord,
and he delights in His way.**

Psalm 37:23

Time

When time crowds in on you --
and you wonder if you can take it any longer ...

> You've got a deadline for a financial note
> that you can't meet .

> You've got a deadline in your business and
> you may have to fold it.

> You've got deadlines with your family and
> you're not keeping the deadlines.

Whatever it may be --
this is what God teaches:
Count your days ... not your months,
your weeks or your years --
but your days on this earth that
you may acquire wisdom toward your Lord ...
who loves you.

It isn't really about *time*.
It's about **eternity**.
The question is: do we *live* that way?

**But as for us, we will bless the Lord from this time
forth and forever. Praise the Lord.**

Psalm 115:18

Conquering the adversity attitude

Is the only blessing in your life encouragement?
Or is it also discouragement? From which do we learn?

Which most logically causes us to turn to the Lord?
In every year there is always adversity ... always
unforeseen ... the very type of adversity where we
could sit down and figure it out in advance.

The Bible tells us in the prophecy of Isaiah that the Lord
Himself sets up adversities against His own people.

Now why would He do that? It's through adversity ...
that we are *spiritually* alert,
that we are *spiritually* corrected,
that we are on target, and we are *spiritually* humbled.

**The Lord is my shepherd I shall not want. Yay
though I walk through the valley of the shadow of
death, I will fear no evil: for Thou art with me; Thy
rod and Thy staff, they comfort me.**

With every adversity I turn more towards Christ.
The more I turn to Christ, the more I trust Him.
The more I trust Christ, the more I love Him.
The more I love Christ, the more I live Him.

Psalm 23:1-4

Are you living on the inside?

The part
we don't understand
about our lives
is that each one of us
is an inside person.

That's where we live ... not on the outside.

My most serious conversations
are never verbalized.
They are talked out
on the inside of my life.

Isn't that the same with you?

All of us know how much easier it is
to live differently on the outside --
than on the inside.

**For He satisfies the longing soul,
and the hungry soul He fills with good things.**

Psalm 107:9

The advantage of delay

There's not a person today who is not blessed
because of the delay in the Messiah in returning.
It's because of His love towards you and towards me.
There is not one of us who doesn't have unbelieving
loved ones, members in our own families and our
closest friends. We should go to our knees and thank
the Lord for His delay, and yet we don't. We become
terribly impatient with the Lord. We wish He would
hurry but He doesn't.

Everyone of us has natural anxieties in our hearts
about the things we don't understand -- the life
that has been taken, the child that doesn't respond,
the closest friend who became an enemy, the
estrangement of the wife or the husband -- all these
things will be understood. And you know what? We
learn to trust the understanding of Christ the longer
we wait.

That's why the Psalmist in an exuberant moment says,
**I waited patiently for the Lord. He pulled me up out
a place of the miry clay, and set my feet upon a rock,
and established my goings.**

I would rather delay 1000 years than to have Him
come today, if it means someone I love might not
otherwise know Christ.

Psalm 40:1-2

Add to your faith

> " I feel like a prisoner of rebellion.
> Can a prisoner free himself?"

No! That's a basic question -- can the prisoner free himself? No!

Every promise of God has to be true.
Every protection of God has to be absolute.
Every blessing of God has to be real.
Otherwise we have no right whatsoever
to believe God.

With every promise God makes, there is a gift ...
and there is always a responsibility.

If God gives you a child, you will have a responsibility
... and difficulty ... and heartache ... and joy ... and
sorrow -- the rest of your natural life.

If God gives you a second chance, you will have the
responsibility to use that second chance quite
differently.

**And beside this, giving all diligence, add to your
faith virtue; and to virtue knowledge.**

II Peter 1:5

Forgiven?

Have you ever had trouble
getting someone to forgive you?

You go to them and you apologize ...
and you are penitent.
You ask their forgiveness.

They may listen intently. Then they may
fold their arms and look at you and say,
      "Yeah. Yeah. Maybe I will come to see it
      your way someday -- but not now."

And you conclude,
      "I am not forgiven."

Really?

Where is sin forgiven -- other than at the Cross?

Do you let a person who will not accept your
penitent heart and extend to you forgiveness --
paralyze you in your Christian life?

Getting refined ... for a unique purpose

Have you ever felt that most of your life has been scrap? I know I have. Have you ever reached the point where you felt totally useless? Is your life strewn with scrap heaps, opportunities missed or misused, time that was not used wisely, love that was spurred, never taken seriously, talents or intelligence never directed toward anything profitable?

That's the wonder of our Lord. This thing we call growth is the work of a God who is described as a consuming fire. The Lord wants to take the scrap heap in your life and mine, melt it down and make it usable.

A retake? My friend, you can have it.
The perfected tape can be spliced into your life --
because the greatest salvage operator in all creation is the Creator Himself, Jesus Christ. He loves you -- not as a pile of rubbish or garbage, not as a heap of junk or trash, but as a unique person created in His image for a unique purpose.

The Apostle Paul, in writing to the Corinthians, said, **Every man's work shall be made manifest: for the day shall declare it, because it shall be revealed by fire; and the fire shall try every man's work of what sort it is.**

I Corinthians 3:13

Lucky

At one time I picked up a paper in the Midwest. I believe it was the Chicago Tribune. I love to read classified ads.

It's the best index to any community -- what they're thinking, what they're charging, what they're going for. The ad read:

> "Lost. A little white French poodle. Full of hair, but mangy. Left ear bitten off. Right eye blind. Left back leg broken. Answers to the name *Lucky*."

Everyone needs confidence ... everyone has to have it. But suppose you have confidence that runs out with age? Suppose you have confidence that runs out when you lose your spouse? Suppose you have confidence that runs out when you lose your job? Or when you lose that special opportunity?

The Apostle Paul is writing to people whose confidence is threatened. They feel a little bit like the poodle, *Lucky*. They're subject to persecution. They're members of a small Christian community that emerged from a persecution situation.

You will guide me with your counsel and afterward receive me to glory.

Psalm 73:24

A battlefield ...

You know ...
we forget our lives are a battlefield.

There's not a one of us
that doesn't have a compulsive sin
in his or her life --
which, in our moments of greatest weakness,
we keep returning to.

We find ourselves reverting
to the man or woman
we used to be ...
to the weakness
we still have ...
and to the sin
we most zealously pursue.

You wonder about the Christian?

I tell you ...
the greatest
discouragement
of the Christian is --
whether the Lord can forgive
this latest thing that I've done
 -- repeating the same old sin.

Discernment is ...

Discernment is taking the knowledge that we have
of the Lord and applying it to the questions we have
of life and death. If you go through life hinging on a
preacher ... or on a church ... or on a Sunday school
teacher ... or on a friend ... for your discernment ...
then you *may* have salvation but you'll never enjoy it,
because all through life you'll be tossed to and fro.

Every wind of doctrine that comes along and everyone
whose cunning and deceitful will tend to deceive you
-- and strip you of the joy and the confidence of your
salvation.

If Christ is to be discerning towards us ...
is it too much to ask that we be discerning
toward Him?

*Lord, give us the discernment from Your viewpoint
rather than the worlds.*

**If God so loved us, we also ought to love one
another ... If we love one another God abides in us
and His love is perfected in us.**

I John 4:11

Did the wisest man make mistakes?

Solomon was embarrassed and for all his wisdom
he was embarrassed by his Lord. In time, Solomon
married, in violation of God's direct Commandment.
He married 700 women indiscriminately. He also
had 300 concubines. Solomon found himself
considering world opinion, as you and I do today --
forgetting that in the world which Solomon lived in,
the world in which you and I live -- the Lord is not
believed. So Solomon ... for all his wisdom ... was
embarrassed by his Lord.

Solomon took into account the value of world opinion.
Solomon found himself embarrassed by the narrowness
of the Lord. With all of his open-mindedness which
became like a sieve, Solomon found it hard to put a fix
on any standard.

It was when he should've been wisest in the latter days
that Solomon turned to false gods of his own pagan
wives. He offered sacrifices. He was embarrassed by
his Lord.

**For we all stumble in many ways. And if anyone
does not stumble in what he says, he is a perfect
man, able also to bridle his whole body.**

James 3:2

Is there importance in being appreciated?

Over 80% of Jesus' teaching is illustration ...
not Scripture. It is explained in common ordinary
things so people could understand.

Have you ever stopped to think that you do not
understand anything you cannot accurately illustrate
... but to accurately illustrate, you must first
understand. It's a real key to explaining, to teaching
and to have communication.

The next time you feel put upon because you're
misunderstood, remember the spit on the face of
Jesus.

The next time you hear words that are misinterpreted
or you are put down, remember one thing:
the jeering throbbing in the ears of Jesus.

The next time you say:
"I don't feel appreciated," --
remember when the God of all this came to earth.
He wasn't appreciated either.
And if you follow Jesus -- this is the person you follow.

**Do not withhold good from those to whom it is due,
when it is in your power to do it.**

Proverbs 3:27

The rich young man

The rich young man comes to Jesus at the height of his youth ... at the crest of his career. Not depending on the actuary tables of the insurance company ... not pretending as so many of our young people today under 30 pretend, that they will never be 31 ... that they'll never be 65 ... that there will always be tomorrow and a young tomorrow. The young man asked this basic question: *What am I going to do to inherit ... to seize ... to lay hold of ...to have as a present possession right now ... eternal life?*

Not this temporary thing ... not this youthful body that's healthy ... not this status that is with my wealth ... not this popularity that I now enjoy ... but *eternal life* that I can always enjoy.

What must I do to have eternal life?

Jesus says:
My friend, before you are willing to come after Me ... before you would take up a Cross ... before you would ever follow, you have to get rid of the god you have inside your life. The obedience of the Commandments that you claim has nothing whatsoever to do with the god that has you ... which, in your particular case, is money.

Mark 10:17

Scapegoat

David (with his 600 men) arrived at the town that has been given to them because they served the Philistine King. It's the town of Ziklag. When they arrived, they find it burned to the ground. They find all their wives, all their sons, all their daughters, are taken captive -- alive. No dead bodies and every possession they have -- gone!

How would you react? The Bible tells us David and all 600 men wept. They wept until they lacked the strength to weep anymore. Then we're told that the hearts of the 600 men were embittered hearts because their sons and daughters had been taken captive.

Suddenly they turn, and they want to stone David. Now this is the one man they serve ... this is the man they have left their own people to follow ... this is the man they've pinned their hopes on for the future ... this is the man God will make King of all Israel ... but they want to stone him.

Why would they want to stone him? *Bitterness always seeks a scapegoat.*

When my heart was embittered ... with Thy counsel Thou wilt guide me.

Psalm 73:21-24

Questions at a social party ...

I want to pose to you these questions:
>How do you and I regard sin?
>How does God regard sin?
>How seriously do you and I regard punishment?
>How seriously does God regard punishment?

You can go to just about any party today. If something is brought up about Jesus Christ in the most casual way, someone will turn and take issue with you.
>"You sound like fire and brimstone. Hell fire and brimstone," people will say to you ... "You don't believe in hell do you?" "Well," you might say, "I figured Jesus told the truth about Heaven. I would find it very difficult to believe He lied about Hell."

Then they respond with a vicious tone in their voice:
>"You can't tell me that a God of love would turn around to someone abused in his childhood, never had an easy life ... and send such a man to hell."
>"No, sir, I couldn't tell you that.
>But Jesus could."

For He spoke, and it was done; He commanded and it stood firm.

Psalm 33:9

Parking your brains

The Lord doesn't want anyone to park his brains
just because he comes to Christ. He wants him to
use his brains because he comes to Christ
... and to learn all he can.

Do you want to understand righteousness?
Then understand evil, and get the contrast with Christ.
Do you want to understand goodness?
Then look at the badness of the earth.
Do you want to understand what it is to be forgiven?
Then look at the guilt ... perhaps in your own heart.

No, you don't have to park your brains to come to
Christ ... but you do have to realize who gave it to you,
and the use for which it was given: to live life,
not to throw it away ... to love, not to hate ...
and to forgive, not to produce guilt.

What a Christ we have! We're to love Him with our
soul ... with all our heart ... and with all our mind.

*God has looked down from the heaven, upon the sons of
men, to see if there is anyone who understands.*

**He restores my soul; He leads me in the paths of
righteousness. For His name's sake.**

Psalm 23:3

Overcoming my doubts

The pagan is far more honest about doubt than the Christian. Christians try to cover up doubt as though doubt is wrong. There's nothing wrong about doubt. John Calvin was a pretty good attorney and he said,

> "You will never find a saving faith without an element of doubt. A saving faith is having a settled mind about the person Jesus, despite your doubts in other areas."

Imagine you're in a *far country* ...
just as the prodigal son.
Disobedient, filled with doubt and anguish ...
doubting you have a Father,
doubting you're a daughter or a son
of the living Lord --
because of disobedience.

The source of *confidence* in my life is
my *obedience* to Jesus Christ.
The source of doubt and lack of confidence in my life
is due to disobedience to Jesus Christ.

That's what God says ... what do you say?

"Have faith in God," Jesus answered.

Mark 11:22

Forgive

Do you realize how many
Christian churches are split
because of unforgiveness?

Do you realize how many
people can validly say --
"I know a number of mean
Christians, mean as snakes --
meaner than any people
I've known as pagans?"

Yeah. Why?
Because they've missed
the whole point of the
Christian faith --
which is forgiveness.
The greatest need in our
lives is met in Christ.
Our role model is Christ.

And even as they spat on him, and jeered at him,
and called him a liar and a fraud -- and challenged him
to come down from the Cross,
He screamed:
My God, forgive them,
they don't know what they're doing.

Luke 23:34

The Holy Spirit

How do you think
spiritual things
are discerned,
understood
and applied in life?

Not by
the intellect of anyone.
Not by
the curiosity of anyone.
But only by
the *Holy Spirit*
working *inside*
the spirit of a man --
which is inside the man.

**Now we have received,
not the spirit of the world,
but the spirit which is of God;
that we might know the things
that are freely given to us of God.**

I Corinthians 2:12

What does it take to make a guy like me grateful?

Corrie Ten Boom and her entire family lived in the
Netherlands during World War II and they happened
to be a Gentile family -- but they hid in their home
and saved more than 100 Jews. The penalty ... the
Germans sent them to a concentration camp and all
the family died there except Corrie, who somehow
survived.

She was speaking one night in West Berlin just after
World War II. When she finished her talk which was on
forgiveness, a German came up to her, and he said,
  "Look at me. Look at me."
And she looked at him and said,
  "I don't know you.
  I've never seen you in my life."
He said, "Then look again."
And suddenly Corrie had flashbacks to the
concentration camp. She knew his face.
He was the guard who had raped her sister and
savaged her -- and her sister had died.

In that moment of truth, Corrie said, "I had to decide
whether the forgiveness extended to me should be
extended through me to this guard who raped my
sister."
And he stared at her. He said,
  "If you forgive me, I'll accept your Christ."
And she said, "I do forgive you."
Then he said, "I accept your Christ."

Discovering Happiness

The Psalmist, in the 103rd Psalm ...
makes this fantastic description of the Lord:
The Lord is compassionate and gracious,
slow to anger and abounding in loving-kindness.
He will not always strive with us,
nor will He keep his anger forever.
There comes a point when even Jesus runs out of
patience and that's a promise!

Doesn't it seem strange when we say:
It's up to us to be happy ... when He keeps saying:
> *It's up to us to be faithful ...*
> *whether we're happy or not?*

Don't you think He gets a little tired
of having died
that we might live --
and then not having us live?

The Lord is *patient* and restrains himself from
coming, even now, at this moment. Why?
So that those still indifferent ...
those still impatient with the Lord ...
those still wondering about His goodness and His
identity, may yet come to the conclusion that
He loves them!

Psalm 103:8-9

Don't give up!

My friend, we are all ashamed when we run out of courage ... and when we run out of faith. But I would remind you that Jesus in the Garden of Gethsemane on the very night when he was betrayed ... He prayed, **My Father, if it is possible, let this cup pass from me.** And the Lord's answer was *No*. In the same week in which He was greeted like a conquering hero, He was crucified ... and in the last statement from the Cross, Jesus said, **It is finished.**

From the moment you come to Christ, it can become very tough. You're out of step with the world. You know that what the world says is right or wrong is not what God says. You may have known great popularity before. Now there are people that avoid you. You may have been very articulate in talking about the secular, but now you've found yourself inarticulate talking about Christ. And you're discouraged. And you say, "I'm just about to give up. I'm not sure it's worth it."

Hang on, my friend. Christ can turn the most desperate life into a life of victory, and of confidence. Remember the promise because it's just as real as the promise of resurrection, forgiveness, and that is this -- that **He who has begun a good work in you will see it through to completion.** It's not where you start, it's where you finish. Don't give up. He'll never throw you aside. He'll always stick with you. And He will eternally love you.

Philippians 1:6

What's your standard?

Whatever you do,
whether it's worship ...
whether it's work ...
whether it's something
you're an expert in ...

whether it's something in which
you have no expertise ...

do whatever you do by one standard --
do it every time for Christ.

Do it by one standard ...
good is not good enough ...
best is not best enough.

Christ is the only standard.

Do you know what
the Apostle Paul says
to the Colossian Christians?

**Whatever you do, do your work heartily
as to the Lord, rather than to men.**

Colossians 3:23

By the action of God ...

By the action of God you are being changed into the
likeness of Christ from glory to glory or -- as Henry
Drummond observes:
  "From character to character."
Let's spell that out.

If you look back in your own life and you were to chart
it, just draw a line down the middle of the page. Put
on the left side of that page every virtue that you have
by your own willpower.

List it.

Then on the other column on the right side of the page
list every virtue that you have in your life ...
those you have acquired from someone else.

You will find the column on the left very short.
You will find the column on the right very long.
Why? Because we acquire our goodness from
what we live and with whom we live.

**But it is good for me to draw near to God; I have put
my trust in the Lord God, that I may declare all Thy
works.**

Psalm 73:28

Does sin deliver?

> "Ben, do you know what it's like to have a
> beautiful 19-year-old tell you at 55 that you
> are the most handsome, the most manly
> person she has ever known?"

The Bible does not deny that there is pleasure in sin.
But the Bible points out that it is always ... only for a
little while. It is always temporary. It is always
something that has deluded you. It never does what
it promises to do. That is why Satan, who brings these
temptations to us, is the father of all lies. But how do
you make choices for Christ? By following. Jesus will
put you out of step with the world. Incidentally, the
world has never been in step. So that's nothing new.

But it is when people pretend there is no pleasure in
sin that others think:
> "You just don't understand."

Sin -- I understand. I have earned a doctorate degree
in sin ... and most of us have. But sin is always just for
a little while. It never delivers.

**Therefore, there is now no condemnation for those
who are in Christ Jesus.**

Romans 8:1

What acceptance means

If Jesus is rejected by man ... not esteemed, not respected, not admired ... then we can't expect much better.

But when Jesus Christ the Lord, the living God, has accepted you ... do you realize what that acceptance means ... if you are accepted by God?

Then you can accept yourself, and you can accept others. Practically the only way the average person finds that out -- despite what he thinks of as the rejection of God and the rejection of himself and the rejection of others -- is through one loving heart who comes in and says:

> "I want to be a brother or sister to you.
> I want you to know that Christ accepts you.
> You can accept yourself, and you can accept others. Despite the difficulty of life, there can be the wonder of it, and the beauty of it, and the confidence."

That's what it's about.

Let the wicked forsake his way, and the unrighteous man his thoughts; and let him return to the Lord, and He will have compassion on him.

Isaiah 55:7

True?

I am trained in doubt.
I am a third generation attorney.
I was CEO of a daily newspaper.
I served in Central Intelligence.

My entire training,
beginning at the dinner table in my home as a child,
was to accept *nothing* on the face of things
but to doubt everything initially.

I have a doubting background.
But I am also pragmatic.
If this Bible alone knows me
and this Bible proves to be true
when I *disobey* or when I *obey* ...
then there is *validity* to the Bible.

You ask,
        "But Ben, why do you believe the Bible

Because every word of the Bible that
I have *disobeyed*
has proved to be true ...
and every word of the Bible
I have *obeyed*
has proved to be *true*.

Fighting through faith

Ezekiel was among those who was a refuge -- captured
and transferred into a foreign land.

How easy it would have been to have felt dejected,
rejected, despised, self-pity.

But Ezekiel makes this statement:
The spirit entered me and set me free on my feet.

That's why part of the Christian faith is fight.
And without fight, you don't have a Martin Luther ...
you don't have a John Calvin ...
you don't have a Billy Graham ...
you don't have great servants of the Lord
down through the years.

Faith is not just what you do ...
but what you can stand.

Faith must have something else.
It has to know that --
no matter what happens --
God is in control.
Jesus is on the throne.

Ezekiel 2:2

Have you lost perspective?

The Apostle Paul is writing to an area in the Middle East ... in the book of Colossians, Chapter 3. There are three towns of some prominence in that area.
One is the town of Colossae. It is located 100 miles from Ephesus, where we know Paul spent some time; it is because of his evangelism, the word which he preached that there are any believers in this little city of Colossae ... and Colossae, is not unlike the society in which we live. It was sophisticated ... it was religious ... it was open-minded ... highly tolerant ... the people could always find room for another idea.

Among the believers of Colossae, the great temptation was the great temptation we see among believers today -- to live the new life in the old way.
> "Ben," you say," how could that possibly happen?"

Because they had lost perspective ... and they had reverted to their old cultural ways ... because the experience of conversion was now a part of history and they were back in the thick of things -- as they were in the real life in the marketplace. In actuality, they had lost their gratitude.

And above all these put on love, which binds everything together in perfect harmony.

Colossians 3:14

The promise of the Cross is ...

Does it surprise you how very few friends we have
when we really need friends?

Jesus says,
*If you ask me, Jesus Christ ... crucified, risen,
ascended and returning ... into your life, I will not
forsake you. I'll be your friend when the weather is
bad ... not just when it's fair.*

*I'll be with you when your decisions are wrong,
or I think they're wrong, and I know them to be
wrong -- because I'm God.*

Is there anything as annoying as an ungrateful person?
Someone you do and do and do for ... then they
thumb their nose at you and
turn in the other direction --
particularly when you
need a friend?
Jesus Christ won't do that.

**For the Lord will not forsake his people for his great
name's sake.**

I Samuel 12:22

Why go to Church?

Well, why go to Church?

If the Word of God,
the Bible,
is not to be trusted ...
you're up the creek ...
and you're wasting your time.

      "But Ben," you say, "I have so many doubts."

From time to time there are things
I don't understand.

Let's get this straight:
Every one of us has areas of our lives
where we can say:
      "Intellectually I understand that, and by
      faith -- they correspond."

But there are other times when we have to say:
      "By faith alone -- I believe that."

**We took sweet council together,
and walked unto the house of God in company.**

Psalm 55:14

Two verses

The guts of the Bible can be found in just two
verses. **For by grace are ye saved through faith, and
that is not of yourselves; it is the gift of God. Not of
works, lest any man should boast.**

And I thought to myself, what is grace? Grace is totally
unmerited, undeserved, unearned and totally at the
initiative of God -- at His pleasure and for His pleasure.
And saved ... what am I saved from? From all the
things I've done wrong. From my guilt. From my past.
And how does that happen? It's the gift of God. I'm
saved from my own sin -- by His love, at His initiative,
by grace -- through faith.

What kind of faith? You say we can do it. I know we
can do it. Optimism is not faith. That's not God's gift.
I've done it before. I can do it again. I've got faith.
That's not God's gift. That's self-confidence.

And what is it by works? No, it's not by works.
Keeping the Ten commandments -- that's works.
Trying to live the Sermon on the Mount -- that's works.
When you have faith, it is My gift. When you try
works, that is your ego. It is not My gift.

That when I answer for my whole life -- I say either
I did it or Jesus did it. And God says, it is My gift and
Jesus did it.

Ephesians 2:8-9

The Cross

On the Cross in the most internal of all things ever
done by anyone since the creation of the universe ...
God ... the Son, in the flesh ...
> *Jesus never lusted* after a man's wife ...
> became adultery ...
> *He never entertained malice* in his heart toward
> another man ... became murder ...
> *He never bent the knee to anyone* but the Father
> ... became idolatry.

The Bible says:
He who knew no sin was made to be sin itself.

Every sin in my life. Every sin in yours. And the
penalty for each of these sins is hell. Nobody got
home scot-free.

That's why the Cross is not a few hours of agony with
nails in the hands. The Cross ... in the mystery of God
... is the most internal moment in all creation.

For the first time in all of eternity God the Son, as
Jesus of Nazareth, is separated from God the Father,
and He endured my hell and He endured your hell.
The price was paid ... and it was paid in full.

II Corinthians 5:21

Expecting what?

What a question I used to ask myself -- what do I hope to get out of life? Good education, good job, good marriage, good family, perhaps grandchildren and lots of fun ... and for how long? 70 - 80 years. Then one day I turned to the flipside and I asked myself the question -- well, what do I hope to get out of death? What do I get out of dying?

Forgiveness. Seeing Jesus face to face.
Being with loved ones, and friends and all believers.
No crying. No tears, no pain, no mourning, no death.
No time, just eternity. No frustration, no disappointments, no sorrow. No hatred, no injustice ...
just the love of God.

Then I began to understand, the flipside of 70 - 80 years on this earth. Then I began to understand a close friend of mine who used to say, "I go to church every other year. One time, but always on the same day." I said, "What day is that?" He said, "Resurrection, Easter." I said, "Are you going to be resurrected?" He said, "I sure am. Don't you know the Bible says there is universal resurrection? Resurrection to be with Jesus, or resurrection to be without Jesus -- but resurrection for everyone."

He said, "That's my hope. That's my confidence." And I began to understand what I expected to get out of this life doesn't compare with what I'll get out of death. No wonder they call it resurrection Easter. Hard to beat!

Temptation versus testing?

James strikes a note about temptation.

> *Never, ever accuse the Lord of tempting you,*
> he writes. *The Lord is not tempted by evil and*
> *the Lord has never tempted anyone.*
>
> "Then there's a difference between temptation
> and testing?" you ask.

There sure is. God didn't start the economic boycott
of these Christians. Certainly being God your Father,
He didn't initiate social rejection of these Christians.
That wasn't the case.

But there were these trials.

Remember, one of the first trials in the Bible was when
Abraham was asked ... in faith ... to offer up his own
son as a sacrifice to God. Then the Lord intervened and
said,
> "No. I know where you stand."

**Count it all joy when you fall into various trials,
knowing that the testing of your faith produces
patience.**

James 1:2-3

Is ego a mistake?

What's the biggest mistake in your life?
Wasn't it when you overestimated yourself, and
underestimated the Lord?

That has been the experience of every woman and
every man who is honest about his individual life.

It is because of mistakes that we can truthfully say
to each other:
> "We can't pretend to be too spiritual;
> we'd be hypocrites if we did.
>
> We can't claim to be too consistent;
> we'd be hypocrites if we did.
>
> We're not the name of the game;
> we would be hypocrites if we said we were."

It's Jesus! ... and He is all in all.

We are absolutely nothing ...
and nothing without Him.

The only way to honor Christ is by
thinking less of yourself and
a great deal more of Him!

How often did I go to an organized church?

Expecting to hear forgiveness --
but I heard condemnation.
Hoping to hear love -- but I heard hatred.
Expecting to be accepted -- but I was excluded.

And then I remembered the apostle Paul in the Bible
said he judged Jesus by appearance and concluded he
was a fraud, a pony, a liar. And Paul was so wrong that
he said -- *I'll never again judge anyone by appearance.*

So often the organized church says to the alcoholic,
"If you straighten up and sober up, then you can come
to Christ."

That's not what the Bible says. The Bible says you
come to Jesus and I'll give you the power and the
direction and the leadership to straighten out your
life.

Our job is not straighten out other people. Our job
is introduce them to the person that can help them
straighten out and who loves them enough to do it
and has the power. He loves us first. He receives us
first. He just says -- *Come, put your trust in me and
I'll begin a good work in you, that I'll see through
to the finish.*

We love him, because he first loved us.

1 John 4:19

How do you grow in Christ?

How do you *mature*?
Most of us wish it was the same way as Bourbon ...
a matter of time ... a matter of being *aged*.
But it doesn't work that way. You can be a new
Christian 75 years old ... and not grow spiritually!
     "Why?"

Because age doesn't have anything to do with it.
It's faithfulness ... it's love ... it's perseverance ...
it's a battle.

Why do you think the Salvation Army ... which is a
denomination of the Lord Jesus Christ ... calls itself
the *Salvation Army*? Because living the Christian life,
which is what the Bible is about, is a battle. It is always
a conflict. There's always pressure. You are always
living in a pressure cooker.

There isn't much R and R.

And the Lord says -- *I know. I count you worthy for the
kingdom of God ... for which you are suffering.*

**He is the one we proclaim, admonishing and
teaching everyone with all wisdom, so that we
may present everyone fully mature in Christ.**

Colossians 1:28

The mystery

When you come to the Lord's Table of Communion
and you celebrate the Last Supper of Jesus with His
Apostles during the Passover ... does the mystery
strike you? You come and you say,
> "I am a sinner and He is without sin. I don't
> know how to live and I don't know how to die."

Jesus Christ knew how to do both.
I come to the communion table trying to *fathom* the
mystery. How could an all-righteous God love me?

How could He send his only Son to take on Himself
my sin and to endure *my hell* and to pay the price
I owe for my life?

You can go to the wisest man on earth and say,
> "Does the Bible make sense?"
If they have read it ... and very often
they haven't ... they will say,
> "Not to me, not to me."
I can't understand a God who would send his Son from
Heaven to endure what He endured on this earth.

**This is love: not that we loved God, but that he
loved us and sent his Son as an atoning sacrifice
for our sins.**

I John 4:10

Commit your way

Commit your way unto the Lord, as He says, and you do delight in Him; He will not only give you the desires of your heart ... **He will bring to pass** what you commit to Him that you could not possibly pull off. We've forgotten that. As a nation we have come to think that the answers are in Washington. They have never been in Washington. They have always been in Heaven and we've come to learn that.

Rest in the Lord and wait patiently for Him.
Think how often we have had to be patient ...
And think how often we have had to wait on Him.

**A little that a righteous man has is better
than the riches of the wicked.**

I guess the greatest adjustment in our lives is when we find out we are not a whale of a success. We haven't made a lot of money. We can't provide for those we love all we would like to provide.

Yet we find that the little that the Lord has given us ... when we delighted in Him ... has been so stretched and so used and so multiplied ... and so blessed, that it's really better than if we had been rich and had more than we could possibly say grace over.

Psalm 37:5-7

His friendship

It's one thing to call Him Savior.
It's wonderful to call Him Lord.

Think how intimate it is
to call Him friend --
and to know that He voluntarily
lay down His life.

Not in theory, but in actuality.
Because of His friendship for you
-- and for me.
He knows my dark side.
He knows your dark side.

Each one of us wonders --
is there any friend I can completely trust
with the darkest secret of my life?
Trust with the brightest yearning of my life?

Yes, Jesus.

**I don't call you servants anymore, because a servant
doesn't know what his master is doing. But I've
called you friends, because I've made known to you
everything that I've heard from my Father.**

John 15:15

How do we get happiness?

The Bible says
happy is the man
who has mercy
on the poor.

Only the wealthy
know that money
doesn't provide
happiness.

For the rest of us,
it's speculation.

... but he that hath mercy on the poor, happy is he.

Proverbs 14:21

Does it fit?

I'll tell you what doesn't fit -- defeat, anguish,
frustration, terror -- none of it fits. Why?
Because though we can't fathom it, Jesus Christ said
-- *I've come to solve the problems in your life.*

You mean in some lives?
No ... in every life ... the sin problem.
Jesus hasn't come to judge you. He's come to *forgive*
you. He came to do what otherwise you'd have to
do for yourself. He paid the sin price and, therefore,
bought you and me.

I thank God for all the things I do not understand --
because it makes it crystal clear at all points. He
is God and I am not. With whatever intellect He has
given me, or experience has given me, or sadness or
joy He has given me -- I cannot fathom how I got this
far.

And you know how you believe that?
The Holy Spirit is quietly reassuring you inside:
        "It's all true. I love you that much."

**For this is my covenant with them,
when I take away their sins.**

Romans 11:27

The unbeliever ... now a believer

"Ben," you ask, "how can you tell the Christian from the unbeliever?"

Very simply ... the direction of his life changes.
What he once enjoyed ... he gets a little cold about it.
What he once did ... for some reason, he hasn't done for a while.

When he reads the Word of God, he
recognizes --
> *these are the words of my Heavenly Father*
> *who loves me and whose only Son would go to*
> *the Cross for an occasion just like this.*

Every time I sin, I fall.
But from Jesus Christ, I have not fallen away.

That's the encouragement for me and for you.

Be of good courage and he shall strengthen your heart, all you who hope in the Lord.

He who calls you is faithful, who also will do it.

Psalm 31:24
I Thessalonians 5:24

Getting closer ...

Every time I sin, I fall. Every time you sin, you fall.
But does that mean you have fallen away from the
Grace of God? From the gift of salvation? If you were
to die at this moment, does that mean you would go
to hell for *unforgiven* sin?

No wonder it's such a sensitive subject. When we read
the Word of God from the lips of Jesus, the Word of
God is sown in certain people and they receive it with
joy. With real enthusiasm. They jump up and down.
They've never been as happy in their lives and their
lives begin to change.

Suddenly they prefer believers to unbelievers.
Suddenly they talk about the things of God and
they're *interested* in the things of God and they are
into the Word of God.

But in time of *affliction* -- such as the sickness of a
child, or in times of persecution which can include
social persecution or death ... they *fall away*.

**Commit your way to the Lord, trust also in Him,
and He shall bring it to pass.**

Psalm 37:5

Taking a look at tolerance …

We were taught that *tolerance* is the most desired trait of the human life.
What is tolerance? My friend, Fred Smith, says it is an *intellectual position* where man seeks to *remove* control from God.
"How's that again?" you ask.

Man's attempt to remove control from God. *Tolerance.*

Some of the most intellectual people on the face of the earth say that no matter what a man worships, no matter how he lives … if he is *sincere,* that is all that matters … never realizing that you can be *sincerely wrong* … which each of us has been time and time again in our lives.

You see, we have substituted *tolerance* for *love.*
Do you know how much easier it is to tolerate someone with whom you differ … than to *love them*?
Than to *get involved in their lives*?
Than to *extend forgiveness?*

Be tolerant of one another and forgive each other if anyone has a complaint against another. Just as the Lord has forgiven you, you also should forgive.

Colossians 3:13

Telling others how you have lived

At one time I sat with a man who had played some *team* golf that afternoon. He and his partner were believers and they played with two men they had never met. This is the kind of thing they enjoy in the pay and play lifestyle in Florida. When they sat down, something came up about the Lord.

> "You know, I've gone to church all my life," one man said. "I go with my wife. She believes all that. And I've given a lot of money to the Church," he said. "You know, quite a bit at a time. I've even served in various capacities. But you know, there's not one iota of it that's true. It's all a lie. I don't believe any of it. I know there is no heaven. I know there is no hell. I know there is not life after death."

The other fellows seem to nod and pretty much agrees with him. Then one golfer called back that afternoon and said,

> "You know, I didn't say anything when you told me about your view of death. But with your permission, I'd love to discuss Jesus Christ." "You don't have my permission," the man promptly replied.

Why would anyone not want to believe in life after death? Very simply this reason: he's ashamed of how he has lived.

Increasing faith!

How does anyone keep his faith? First of all, he has to develop a conscience for Christ -- attune to what pleases Him and what doesn't please Him, reacting as though this hurts Christ ... reacting as though this exalts Christ.

That's hard to do. That's a new type of conscience -- not what is morally right, but is right by the standards of Christ ... totally new standards.
    "What kind of conscience is that?" you ask. We also have to develop within ourselves the awareness that it's not always what we do ... but what we can stand. There are many of us ready, willing and able to perform services for Jesus Christ and that's what we're able to do.

When the pressure comes ... the pressure of *unpopularity*, of *rejection*, of being *despised* by someone who once loved you or of being misunderstood and seemingly out of step with the rest of the world -- often it's more than we can stand. And faith that finishes is faith that learns not only what to do -- but when to stand.

For whatsoever is born of God overcomes the world ... and this is the victory that has overcome the world ... our faith.

I John 5:4

How to please God

King Solomon. He was a grown man. He was not a
weakling. He was a strong man. He was not a man
without potential. He was a man with great potential.
Yet in his humility, he cries out in prayer to God,
**I am but a little child; I do not know how to go out
or come in. Give me discernment to tell the
difference between what is good and what is bad.**

The Bible tells us that this man pleases the Lord in his
prayer. Solomon hasn't asked for riches, hasn't asked
for a long life, hasn't asked for revenge against his
enemies.
God said to him,
*Because you haven't asked for these things, I'm
going to give you an understanding heart. I'm going
to add to that heart what you haven't asked for.
I'm going to give you riches. I'm going to give you
honor. There will be no king in your time like you.
And I want to offer you one thing more ...
I will give you long life if you walk in my ways
and keep my commandments and observe my
judgments.*

The reaction of Solomon? The reaction is to rise to
worship and, in gladness of heart, to make a feast for
his servants.

I Kings 3: 7-14

What is a "sign"?

A sign is a miracle that advertises itself
to inform people of the truth of God --
not just a miracle. Let's get that straight.
At a wedding Jesus shortcuts the entire process
and goes directly from water to wine.
> "That's a miracle," you say.
That's right ... He short-circuits!

What did it do? It met a need ... a need at a little out
of the way wedding party. 15 years later I'm sure no
one would've remembered the party. Whatever
happened, just a little need in the life of a groom.
An embarrassment. **They have no more wine**,
Mary simply says.

She doesn't make any request of Jesus. She just
informs Him that they're out of wine, thinking He
will perhaps declare at this moment that He is the
Messiah! Instead, He supplies the need. We are told
that this was the first sign in His public ministry.

What does this miracle say?
> I have power over nature.
> I have power to transform water into wine.
> I have the power to intervene in the normal
> process of life and to meet the need in the life
> of this single groom.

John 2:3

How long does it take?

Why does it take so long to mature?
Maturity is supposed to be the name of the game.
Why's it so difficult?

Why is it that so many of us can say, after 10 years:
>"I don't really know God any better.
>I don't really trust Him anymore.
>I don't really understand Him any better.
>And my feelings for Him are not as deep
>as the night I confessed to Him?"

How long does it take?   What's missing?

Why does Jesus say,
**I have come that you might have life and have it
more abundantly.**

Then after 10 years as a confessing Christian,
is your life anything but abundant?
Is it all a lie?
Or is there something you have missed?
Something you never quite understood?

Have you ever thought to yourself:
>"Just a little more proof and I will believe?"
Are you waiting for a sign?

John 10:10

How many people have not disappointed you?

You know discouragement
is the closest thing to pride
that we have --
but remember ...

> All the water in the world can't sink a ship
> unless the water gets inside the ship.
>
> All the disappointments in life cannot
> sink your soul or mine unless we allow
> it to seep in -- and to become
> discouragement about the ultimate
> goodness of God.

Jesus loves me this I know;
for the Bible tells me so.

With the automatic confidence in the goodness of
God, and his only Son, Jesus, I've tried to separate
more and more ... what is disappointment ...
and what is discouragement.
Think about it!

And this hope will not lead to disappointment ...

Romans 5:5

Tired of waiting?

Do you know what it's like to wait? Tell a child he's going to do something Saturday. That's an eternity to wait, particularly if it's at the beginning of the week. But even on Friday, it seems like an eternity to a child.

Moses had been up on the mountain only 40 days and 40 nights. Coming down from the mountain, Moses asked,
   What happened?

He looks around him. Everyone is eating ... everyone is drinking and everyone is apparently involved in sex. There's a golden calf, and right before it is an altar -- incense has been burned.

So much of the discouragement in the Christian life is the Lord making us *wait.*

We want to know when -- and He doesn't tell us.
We want Moses now -- and he doesn't come.
We want it to happen now -- and it doesn't happen now. Do we get impatient and, just like the Hebrews, we give up?

Wait for the Lord; be strong and let your heart take courage. Yes, wait for the Lord.

Psalm 27:14

The refining process includes ...

Whenever I talk to an older person who doesn't know Christ, I usually can see in his eyes a sorrow as he says to himself,

> "I'd like to do it over, but I'm so filled with scrap. I've made a mess of it. I'm too old to do it over. I wish I'd taken the time. I wish I'd dealt with Christ. I wish I hadn't botched my marriage, my career, my friendships. I'd like to do it over but I know I can't."

Today you may be 30 or 80, and you've never come to the Lord. You say,

> "Oh, if I could only start over again."

My friend you can. Now, with the wisdom of age, with years of experience -- you can come to Christ. He will melt you down and remake you ... a **new creation** as Paul says.

The refining that needs to be done ... getting rid of the old scrap ... the Lord will do. He does it through affliction. He does it through trials. He does it by fire.

The Apostle Peter in his first letter writes:
... that the trial of your faith, being much more precious than of gold that perishes; though it be tried with fire, might be found unto praise and honor and glory at the appearing of Jesus Christ.

2 Corinthians 5:17
I Peter 1:7

Do I really matter?

I've struggled with that for so many years.
My friend telephoned and he said,
"Man, I lost my job, my retirement fund, our house --
and then I lost my wife. I know I don't matter."

I was in the emergency room one night and I saw a man
that I knew rather casually. I liked him. He was an active
alcoholic, great salesman and he mumbled that he had
taken a butcher knife and tried to slash his throat and he
said, "Except for the fact that it was dull -- I wouldn't be
here. Nobody cares whether I live or die."

I looked him right in the eye and I said,
"Robert, I don't know you well -- but I care."
        He said, "Do you really?"
I said, "Yeah."

        He said, "Then I won't try it again."
Something that night happened I've never understood.
He never had another drink that I know of and he lived
out a normal life. The Bible, if it's to be believed, says that
one little bird -- a sparrow -- doesn't fall to the ground
that God doesn't note it and permit it and care about it.

Do I really matter? The Bible points to the Cross where
the full penalty for my life was paid. Jesus endured my
hell. He went to Hell for me when I didn't even think
there was a God. Now He had my attention. Now I
realize I really do matter. What about you my friend?
What do you think about whether you matter.

Don't you judge me!

Boy, the question plagued me. How was I to know what was right and what was wrong when the Bible itself said I was not to judge. Well, it's popular to play God. It's popular to want to straighten out the other guy -- to reinforce your own judgment by saying I'm not to judge. The Bible says I'm not to judge.

But you know, I guess of all people I've known, I have known Satan the best and I sure have known him longer. And wherever words are possibly double or triple in meaning, I tend to look and see why Satan wants me to judge, then to pull back on the Bible and to say, "It's ok . I know I'm not to judge. Otherwise I'll be judged."

There's so much in my life I judged -- other people by their appearance, their grammar, their articulation -- until one day I knew a man rather well who spoke with bad grammar. Oh man, he butchered the King's English. But then I realized he was twice as smart as I will ever be. And then I remembered King David in the Bible had a prophet that came to him and told him a story of a man who had one little lamb -- and the rich man came and took away that man's lamb. And King David judged and was immediately incensed and he said, "This man should surely die and he shall repay fourfold." The prophet looked at David and he said, "You're the man. You didn't take a lamb -- you took a man's wife."

Forgiving

Why should anyone forgive you —
when you've done something perfectly horrible
to them?

I'll tell you why.
The Christian Church is suppose to be in the
business of forgiveness —
not condemnation.
It tried condemnation for centuries.

God has never given over judgment to
the Christian Church.
Judgment is reserved to Jesus Christ alone.

And Christians have to be in the business
of forgiving.

Why?
Because such an awful cost was paid for every
forgiveness -- the blood of Christ on the Cross ...
for the casual and the really difficult things
no man without Christ can find in his heart to forgive.

**For if you forgive men when they sin against you,
your Heavenly Father will also forgive you.**

Matthew 6:14-15

BEN HADEN

BEN HADEN

Speaker
Changed Lives
changedlives.org
1968 ... going forward for years
to come. Ben Haden passed away
October 24th, 2013.

Pastor
First Presbyterian Church
Chattanooga, Tennessee

Key Biscayne Presbyterian Church
Miami, Florida

Author

Vice President, General Manager
Kingsport Times-News
Kingsport, Tennessee

CIA Security Operative
Korean War

President
Long Oil Company

Washington & Lee School of Law
University of Texas

changedlives.org

Books by Ben Haden

I See Their Faces

Rebel to Rebel

2 Bit Prayer Life

Why? The Tough Questions

Why II? The Tough Questions

Let's Talk About It

Forgiven

Ben Haden Teaches Colossians

Why not Chuck It?

Do You Have A Yo - Yo Faith?

What is God Like?

Is God ...?

Will I Live After I Die?

ONE on ONE

❷NE on ONE